Table of Contents

Chapter One ....
Chapter Two 7
Chapter Three 15
Chapter Four 21
Chapter Five 28
Chapter Six 34
Chapter Seven 40
Chapter Eight 47
Chapter Nine 53
Chapter Ten 60
Chapter Eleven 66
Chapter Twelve 73
Chapter Thirteen 79
Chapter Fourteen 85
Chapter Fifteen 92
Chapter Sixteen 99
Chapter Seventeen 106
Chapter Eighteen 112
Chapter Nineteen 119
Chapter Twenty 126
Chapter Twenty-One 132
Chapter Twenty-Two 139
Chapter Twenty-Three 145
Chapter Twenty-Four 152
Epilogue 159

© Copyright 2023 by Erica Frost All rights reserved.

IN NO WAY IS IT LEGAL to reproduce, duplicate, or transmit any part of this document in either electronic means or in printed format. Recording of this publication is strictly prohibited and any storage of this document is not allowed unless with written permission from the publisher. All rights reserved.

Respective authors own all copyrights not held by the publisher.

Ruthless Billionaire

By: Erica Frost

Foreword

Getting mixed up with your ex's older brother is never a good idea. Especially if that ex has been accused of a crime... murder, no less. But crime is my profession. Well, solving it. The moment I step into the reality of the adult world, I feel like I've been thrown into a whirlwind.

My ex's brother never liked me. I actually think he's partly the reason why my ex broke up with me. Now, this billionaire bad boy needs my help. I just want to find out the truth. That's what brings us close, initially. I know why he needs me. I know it can't be anything other than fake love, and us turning from enemies to lovers is just a game.

I know this. But why do I find myself falling for him? Why do I want him to be innocent, with all my heart?

Ruthless Billionaire

Chapter One

Grace

"Where is he?" the man in front of me thunders angrily, without even looking at me properly, his eyes focused on the door to my boss' office. "You get him on that fucking phone and tell him to come here, right now!"

At first, I'm not sure if he recognizes me or not. Because I sure recognize him. It would be very hard not to, because this is the man who was partly responsible for getting my heart broken by none other than his own brother.

"Mr. Stanton," I remind myself that I am at my workplace here, and although I would gladly call him a number of other names, I refrain from doing so. "I cannot do that, because Mr. Jennings is out with a client of ours."

I like the sound of that ours. I am just a secretary in Mr. Jennings' detective office, but I've been here for over a year now, and I've already gotten a small raise, which has made me very proud. I suppose that would mean nothing in the eyes of a financial giant such as Jesse Stanton. In my mind, I refuse to refer to him as a mister, for the very simple reason that he is anything but a gentleman.

He rakes his fingers through his hair. Against all better judgment, I have to admit that he looks even better than he did two years ago when I last saw him. His square jaw is now cleanly shaven, his hair sleek, combed backwards, cut more thinly to the sides. He smells like a man ought to smell.

Too good.

I quickly banish the thought and revert to my professional persona. If he doesn't show that he recognizes me, I won't be the first one to mention it.

"When is he coming back?" he demands. He's still focused on the door behind me, almost as if he half-expects my boss to come out and ask about all this commotion, exposing me as a liar. Well, tough luck.

"I cannot be sure," I chirp back, enjoying this far more than I ought to. Jesse Stanton is used to getting his way. Always. The thought of being the one to refuse him whatever it is he wants brings me so much joy. "I could tell him to call you back when he arrives or if you want to leave a message..."

At that point, he tilts his head at me, as if he's just noticed something about me.

"So, you're not in the habit of helping people you know?" he asks, frowning, without even acknowledging me as a person up until a moment ago. But that's how he always was. You are invisible to him, until the moment you become useful, and not a moment sooner.

"Of course, I am," I reply calmly.

He looks at me expectantly. I tilt my head at him.

"But I can't help you now," I shrug, loving the accented word in my statement.

"Or you don't want to," he corrects me.

"You're asking me to be unprofessional," I grimace at him with displeasure. "Is that what you ask of your own employees as well?"

I don't like him, and it's obvious. Fortunately, the feeling is mutual. The tension in the air is so thick, I could cut it with a knife.

"I advise them on what they should do, like I'm advising you now," he says, with a slight tone of threat. But he doesn't scare me.

I always liked how fate arranged these situations in such a way that you get a chance to prove to some asshole from your past that he didn't manage to break you. Well, this was one of those situations and I was relishing every moment of it.

"You mean, like you convinced your brother I wasn't good enough for him?" I remind him with a slick smile.

Now, I was more than satisfied about putting on a little more make up this morning, just for the heck of it. And my dress felt unusually good on my skin as he traversed my upper body with his gaze, while I sat at my desk.

"I merely pointed out things that you weren't compatible in," he told me, as if revealing a long-kept secret. Not that I cared about any of those explanations now.

What I did care about was the reason behind him barging into Mr. Jennings' detective agency and demanding to be seen, although my boss told me he'd be gone all morning.

"I wasn't dating you," I remind him. "So, I think that it was he who was supposed to decide what we were or weren't compatible in."

"And he did," he shrugs. "I didn't force him to do anything."

"You didn't have to," I answer, but then I realize that he's pulled me into having this conversation and I probably seem still invested in all of this. "Anyway, that is all water under the bridge," I smile at him, using my most professional smile. "Like I said, Mr. Jennings will be out all morning and he can't come back... for anyone." I add that last part more for my sake than for his. "Would you care to leave a message?"

"He's taken on the Romero case?" he suddenly asks, towering over my desk and resting against the polished surface with his open palms. I don't like it that I have to lift my chin to look up at him, but I refuse to get up.

"I'm afraid I cannot discuss an ongoing investigation," I explain, as I was taught to do from the first moment I came here.

He grins. "So, he has."

I bite my lip. I answered him without wanting to. Dammit.

I only glanced at the name on the file that still rested on Mr. Jennings' desk. It was the top one, and the name caught my attention. Lucy Romero. That was the girl's name. The dead girl's name. The DA called about it personally this very morning, and that assured me that this was someone important. Only, I've never heard of her. Why was she so important then?

"Will you be leaving a message, Mr. Stanton?" I ask, focusing on the matter at hand.

"Why do you insist on calling me that?" he frowns unexpectedly.

"Isn't that your name?" I ask, resisting the urge to chuckle.

"You know me."

"So?" I ask. "I'm not awkwardly stumbling onto you in your brother's apartment. This is my place of employment, and I shall address you with courtesy. Now, as for how much of that courtesy you deserve, that is something else."

In my mind, this sounds like an insult. A direct one, to be exact. But he grins.

"You know, I actually like it better when you call me Mr. Stanton," he adds, still grinning.

Somehow, he takes control over the situation, because I'm at a loss for words. That grin awakens naughty thoughts in me, and they have no room in my head. I don't know what to say. My stomach churns, reminding me that it might be high time to end this conversation, before matters get worse.

"Good," I resume my professional persona. "I will be happy to give Mr. Jennings a message that you came looking for him regarding the Romero case. He will contact you, I'm sure."

He instantly pulls away, as if my desk somehow scorched him.

"It is urgent that I speak to him," he tells me in a way that made me forget all about us being enemies.

This wasn't him asking or ordering. This was him pleading. Jesse Stanton was pleading to speak to my boss as soon as he could. I thought pigs would fly before I saw something like that happen.

"I will let him know it's very urgent then," I nod.

I've always been taught not to kick a man while he's down, and somehow, Jesse Stanton seems to be exactly that. Only, I can't figure out why the urgency. And what does he have to do with the dead Romero girl? Was she his girlfriend? Jesse Stanton has had many girlfriends, so it wouldn't be a surprising fact.

I remember the tone of voice. Pleading.

Someone more important than just a girlfriend? A fiancée maybe?

"Have him call me," he adds, sliding his pearl-colored business card across the desk, over to me. I don't reach for it. At least, not before he pulls his hand away.

I just nod. He doesn't say anything. I guess expecting a thank you or a goodbye from Jesse Stanton is too much.

Then, unexpectedly, he turns around at the door. "I didn't tell him to dump you, you know. That mistake was all on him."

And with that mind-blowing sentence he walks out the door, leaving me completely shocked.

Bobby has always been so influenced by his older brother. Jesse's word was law. Bobby would rather die than disobey him. So, when Jesse started telling Bobby I wasn't right for him, I knew this was the beginning of the end, as it was.

Now, I hear this.

I quickly turn my focus to my laptop screen, opening the newest edition of the local newspaper. I don't have to skim through any of the articles. What I'm looking for is on the front page.

Billionaire a murder suspect.

I swallow heavily as my eyes dart left to right, reading the article. The Romero girl is the victim. And the suspect is none other than Jesse Stanton.

My mind is still a blur when the next client walks in, and I give them the same run through as with Jesse. Mr. Jennings' is out and won't be back all morning. They just nod, thanking me, saying they'll come back in the afternoon then.

When I'm left alone, Jesse is the only thing on my mind. That's why he came here asking for my boss. He's a suspect.

I run into my boss' office, grabbing the file. I know I shouldn't be doing this, but curiosity wins over. I start ingesting the info hungrily.

Dead girl... billionaire's weekend getaway home... parties... no clues... no intruders... no murder weapon...

Apart from the girl being found dead on his property, there was nothing else to tie him to the crime. However, that in itself was more than enough sometimes.

I close the file, placing it back on the desk. I know Jesse. Not well, but I know him. And I also know that me having any contact with him isn't good. It isn't right.

I need to help my boss focus on the truth, and we can't have that if the suspect is breathing down our necks. I walk back out to my desk, picking up Jesse's business card. It even smelled like him.

I hesitate for a moment, then tear it up, throwing it into the trash.

It's for the best, I try to convince myself.

Chapter Two

Jesse

"Did you see the news today?" Bobby asks, storming into my office, just as I'm in the middle of a meeting with one of my regional managers.

We both look in his direction, and only then does Bobby realize I'm not alone.

"Sorry, I..."

I grind my teeth, knowing that he wouldn't usually do this. He knows better than that. But the news from this morning must have shocked him, just like they shocked me.

"I'll come back later," he tells me, about to leave, but I stop him.

"Stay," I say. "We're done anyway." I turn to Donoghue, who has also already gotten up, obviously getting the hint. "Let me know how things go."

"Will do," Donoghue, a man in his late fifties, with a suit that made his skin complexion look too ashy, shook my hand. He's never been the one to dress well, but he's been working for my company for over ten years.

We wait for him to close the door on the other side, and then Bobby turns his attention to me.

"What's going on, Jesse?" he asks, sounding petrified.

"All hell's breaking loose, that's what's happening," I say cryptically, raking my fingers through my hair. "I get a call from the fucking cops this morning, saying they got an anonymous tip about a party being held at the Maroon Villa, so they barged in and found that girl... Lucy... dead."

I never thought I would be telling a story like this to anyone. It just seems too... unreal.

"I've already been to the police station, and they didn't say it in those exact words, but I'm not supposed to leave town," I add. "I already canceled my trip to Shanghai scheduled for next week. I'm guessing I'll have to do the same with the Paris trip at the end of the month."

I walk over to my desk, extracting the drawer and taking out an elegant box of Treasurer Luxury Black cigarettes.

"I thought you quit," Bobby frowns at me, as he watches me light up one of them.

I inhale deeply, allowing the smoke to permeate my being. Only then do I reply. "I thought so, too. But then a dead girl turned up at my villa, which I haven't visited in months, and now, I'm the main fucking suspect."

I take another puff, tasting that pure Virginia tobacco that's expensive enough to break anyone's back. Well, anyone's but mine. I get them for free, courtesy of the owner himself. Not that it's anyone's business.

"Do you know the girl?" Bobby asks.

"No," I shake my head, walking over to the window and opening it. Immediately, the commotion of the busy street all the way down hits me. There are both ups and downsides to having your building in the middle of the city center. "I've never seen her in my life."

"So, you don't know how she ended up at the villa?"

I frown at him. "Are you saying I brought her there and then forgot about it?"

"No, no," he shakes his head at me. "Of course, I'm not saying that."

I sigh. "I know. It's just... this has got me worried. I don't know what to do with the cops breathing down my neck."

"What are you going to do?" he asks me.

I consider mentioning that his ex-girlfriend works for the private detective who's working with the district attorney on this case. In a way, that doesn't really matter. What does matter is the fact that I do have a plan.

"I'm not exactly sure," I admit, taking another puff, and allowing the soothing aroma to wash over me. "I need to find out what the cops know about the case."

He pauses for a moment. "I doubt they'll just tell you what you want to know."

"Of course, they won't," I agree. "But I have other sources of information."

I remember Grace and how she wasn't very happy to see me. I guess I can't blame her. I always thought she was a gold-digger. I guess that's why I pushed my brother to break up with her, thinking that someone as beautiful and as clever as her could never love my brother just for himself. There had to be more to this story. A hidden agenda of sorts.

I never really found out whether I was right or not. Bobby decided that he would no longer keep dating her, and he broke up with her. I thought that would be the end of all that. However, it seemed I was wrong.

The moment I saw her sitting in that office, I recognized her. But the concern and fear about what happened didn't let me start with that. I demanded to see her boss, but she was in the way... whether willingly or not. She seemed a little too glad to deny my request.

"Will the cops want to talk to me, too?" Bobby suddenly asks.

His pale blue eyes are wide with fear. He's always been the weaker of the two of us. I don't know if that has anything to do with the fact that he's always been mom's favorite. It used to bug me as a kid. While I was self-sufficient and confident, he was always the one who shouldn't climb trees because he might fall, or he shouldn't ride his bike because he might scrape his knee. I, on the other hand, did all those things and while she did kiss my scraped knee or elbow and put a bandaid on it, that would be the end of that. With Bobby, there would be endless cuddles, hours of compassion, ice cream for dinner... that sort of thing.

I force myself to return to the present moment and to my brother who has always depended on me, and especially so since our parents' death.

"Probably," I say, not wanting to lie to him.

"What should I say?" he asks. I can see him cracking his fingers, something he always did when he was nervous or caught lying. Needless to say, Bobby is the last person you'd want to have lie for you.

I chuckle, unable to refrain from doing so. "You tell them the truth, Bobby. OK?"

"The truth is that we didn't know her," he says simply, as if to practice for when he actually has to say it.

"Exactly," I nod, walking over to him and placing my hand on his shoulder reassuringly. "It'll be fine. I don't know what happened, honestly. Neither of us has been there in months, so anyone could have broken in somehow. I don't know." I don't sound very convincing, but that is because I'm not convinced myself of what happened.

"But wouldn't the security company have proof of that?" he asks.

"I suppose," I frown, already feeling a headache coming on. "The worst thing is that there was no sign of any break in. That means someone unlocked the door."

This is the part that is the most damning. Anyone who knows me also knows that I'm very careful regarding who has access to my home. Or homes, for that matter. Only Bobby has the keys to my every home, just like I have to his. It's something we always did, even before I built my empire. But I don't think telling anyone that Bobby is the only other person with the keys would be a good idea.

I sigh heavily, extinguishing the cigarette in a crystal ashtray on the mahogany desk, without even finishing it. I've lost the will for it.

"This feels like a nightmare," I admit, with that burden pressing heavily upon me. "I keep hoping that I will wake up one morning, and realize that this was all a horrible dream, and that luckily, everything is alright."

"I know," he says, sympathetically. "And it had to happen now."

I inhale deeply, squeezing the bridge of my nose. Sometimes, the displacement of pain from your soul to a physical part of your body works wonders for focus. This time, it helps very little.

"Do you want to go together?" I suggest.

I know that our parents' wedding anniversary was two days ago. I've been meaning to go visit their grave, but first it was work, then this.

"I already went," he informs me.

Of course, I think to myself. The ever dutiful son, unlike me. But I don't say it out loud, because it's not fair.

"Do you want to come with me?" I ask. "You know I don't like going on my own."

That's also true. I always feel like I'm somehow imposing there. I don't know what to say. To be honest, I don't even know if they're listening. I go there, bring a nice bouquet of flowers. Lilies, mom's favorite. And I pour a glass of some good whiskey for dad. I stay there for a few minutes. That's as much as I can handle being there. Then, I run away, like a thief in the night.

"Sure," he smiles, nodding.

When he comes, it's different. He knows how to connect us all. He still knows that. So, I allow him to lead every time he's there. In every other aspect of my life, I'm the leader. But when it comes to expressing my emotions, it's not familiar ground. I'd rather stay in the shadows on that one.

"When do you want to go?" he wonders.

"Tomorrow?" I suggest.

"Sure," he agrees. "Pick me up when you're done."

"OK," I smile.

I appreciate what he's done. He managed to shift my thoughts from what happened to something more natural, something that we do on a monthly basis. For one brief moment, I wasn't focused on the fact that a dead girl was found in my villa and that the only reason I'm not in custody is the fact that they don't have any evidence that I did it.

Bobby waves at me, then leaves my office. It is still early in the afternoon, but I know I don't have any time to waste. Not if I want to go ahead with my plan. Grace's boss probably won't want to talk to me about the case. I don't know him at all, and my name probably means nothing to him. I don't have any ace up my sleeve with this man.

However, with Grace, it might be a different story. I know her. I know how she functions. I know her likes and dislikes. I could find a way for her to share what she knows with me using the oldest trick in the book. It doesn't make me feel that good about myself, but I'm facing life in prison here. All bets are off. I have to find a way to prove to the cops that I didn't do it, and the only way I can manage that is to find out who did.

But first things first.

I grab my cell phone and dial the usual flower shop I work with. They've sent many bouquets on my behalf over the past couple of years.

"Amaretto Flower Shop, how may I help you?" a sweet voice chirps from the other side. I recognize it immediately.

"Hi Sonya, this is Jesse Stanton," I greet her.

I've never seen her, but we've spoken enough over the phone for me to recognize when it's her speaking and when it's the other girl, Marina.

"Oh, hello Mr. Stanton," she purrs back from the other end of the line. "The usual?"

The usual was a combo of roses, bows, a shitful of decorations, making it look like the best damn bouquet a lady had ever received. I like to stay memorable like that... in every way.

"Not this time," I surprise even myself with these words, when I was sure that I planned on just agreeing with her suggestion.

"Oh?" she wonders. "Something special...

"What did you have in mind?"

Somehow, sunflowers would not leave my mind. I frown at the thought. Sunflowers were not even flowers. They were... a snack. But something told me that they would be perfect for Grace. I remember Bobby getting her roses and while she was grateful and smiled at them, I could tell they weren't her favorite flowers. Maybe sunflowers aren't either, but it's worth a shot.

"I want sunflowers this time," I tell her.

"Sunflowers," she repeats. I don't hear surprise in her voice. "We have something called the Morning Garden, a cheerful sunflower design, with a small addition of snow peas and phalaenopsis orchids in bloom, along with coffee beans and eucalyptus."

"Coffee beans?" I ask, not able to imagine what this would look like. "I was actually thinking of something much simpler."

"Oh," she sounds a bit disappointed. "Maybe just a few sunflowers with a nice green silk bow?"

"Perfect," I nod, smiling.

"That's quite different from your usual order, if I may add. That's why I offered something equally complex, with sunflowers," she sounds apologetic.

"Your suggestion was lovely, Sonya," I assure her. "I just need it for... a friend."

"Oh," she seems to understand perfectly this time. "We'll make it very friendly then."

"I'd appreciate that," I grin, leaving Grace's name and workplace, which she immediately puts down. "I want the card to say "Dinner tonight?" and just my initials."

"Of course, Mr. Stanton. Thank you. Will that be all?"

"Yes," I confirm.

"Alright, then. It will be delivered within the hour, as always, unless you have other instructions?"

"No," I confirm again. "That's it."

"Alright," she repeats. "Pleasure doing business with you, as always. Goodbye," she chirps.

"Thanks. Bye," I reply, hanging up the phone.

By the time I go back there this evening, she would have already gotten the flowers. And that is just the first step to my plan.

Chapter Three

Grace

"Grace Watson?"

The man approaches me, carrying the sweetest looking bouquet of sunflowers. For a moment, I thought I recognized him, but on second glance, I realize that isn't the case. Besides, usually the people coming in are looking for my boss, never for me. That is why I immediately assumed he knows me from somewhere.

"Yes, that's me," I smile at him, curious as to where this would lead.

"These are for you," he says, handing me the flowers.

"Oh, thank you," I reply, accepting them in surprise. "Who are they from?"

"There's a card," he points at the flowers, then without any other word of explanation, he waves me goodbye and leaves.

He disappears as quickly as he appeared, leaving me all aflutter with the bouquet in my hands. Who could they be from? I haven't been seeing anyone, although my mom would really like that kind of news. Sadly, I've been too busy to hang out with my friends, who keep partying, as social media keeps proving to me every weekend. They keep inviting me to join them, but I feel so exhausted by the time the weekend comes, that I just want to snuggle up with a good book and read the weekend away. That means that there is absolutely no way a suitor is sending me these flowers. Then, who?

I take the card and read what it says.

Dinner tonight?

J.S.

I immediately feel like someone punched me in the stomach. Then, I feel an onslaught of butterflies trying to get out any way possible.

Dinner? I think to myself. You gotta be joking me. I crumple up the card, throwing it in the trash, where his torn business card is.

I get up, still with the flowers in my hand. I don't need them. I don't want them.

But I can't very well throw them in the trash. Everyone will ask me about them. So, I walk down the hallway, hoping to stumble onto the nice cleaning lady who works here. I don't find her even after fifteen minutes of looking for her, so I head to the kitchen to inquire. In the kitchen, I'm told she's gone down to the janitor's office. Patiently, I follow, waiting for the elevator, and heading down.

I find her exactly where they told me.

"Christina?" I call out to her, as she's with her back to me.

"Yes?" she says, in her eastern-European accent, that can't pronounce soft sounds without revealing where she's from.

"You like flowers, don't you?" I ask, with a smile.

She seems surprised, but she nods.

"Here, for you," I say, offering her the bouquet.

"For me?" she echoes.

"Mhm," I confirm. "You've been doing such a good job, we wanted to show you how much we appreciate it."

"Oh my... I don't know what to say," she replies, pressing her hand to her chest.

I feel a little guilty that the initial purpose of this bouquet wasn't that, but it's made her so happy and I really don't want them. So, it's better this way.

"You don't have to say anything," I smile. "Just keep doing such a swell job. Oh, and say hello to that sweet little girl of yours."

"I will, thank you," she still seems incredulous at what happened.

But I don't stay around, knowing that I have to get back to work. I sit down at my desk a few minutes later, trying to focus, but it's impossible. I can't get Jesse Stanton out of my mind. And then the flowers.

I stare at the screen of my laptop, but nothing happens. My fingers want to type. My eyes want to read. But my brain refuses to cooperate.

I keep thinking about our meeting this morning, and how I was affected by seeing him more than I should have been. Strangely enough, it wasn't Bobby I was thinking about. The truth was that I was heartbroken by him leaving me, because I thought I truly loved him. However, as time went by, I realized that it was simply a very convenient relationship. It was easy to be with Bobby, because he's a nice guy who will agree with everything, even if he sometimes doesn't think it's right. It's just how he is. So, being with him was sheer convenience.

Then, when he left me, I realized that I was indeed happier without him and, more importantly, I need someone who will challenge me every once in a while, instead of agreeing with me on everything. Not that I'm looking for anyone right now. I'm trying to focus on my career path and reaching my professional goals.

Then, Jesse Stanton had to walk into this exact office and make everything confusing somehow.

The door to my boss' office suddenly pops open and he gestures to me to come.

"The Romero case," he tells me, just after I close the door. "I'll need you to call the DA and arrange a meeting for tomorrow."

"Of course," I nod.

"And I don't think I need to tell you that we have to be really careful about this," he sighs heavily, taking off his glasses and rubbing his eyes. He puts them back on after a few seconds. "The press is gonna have a field day with this."

"Well, no one's called yet," I try to comfort him, immediately biting my tongue, because I don't want to tell him that Jesse was here, asking for him.

"I'd say let's hope it stays that way, but I doubt that will happen," he tells me honestly. "Just make sure nothing leaves this office, Grace. It's of the utmost importance for the investigation."

"And Jesse Stanton is the main suspect?" I ask, unable to hold my tongue.

"He is," he nods, grabbing the file and opening it. It was filled with documents, copies and prints.

"Does it look like he's guilty?" I ask again.

He lifts his head to face me. "Other than the fact that the girl was found dead on his property, there is nothing tying him to the crime. Apparently, he was home alone that night. The night watchman verifies that he entered the building around nine in the evening. However, that doesn't mean that he couldn't have left unnoticed."

"Of course," I nod.

"You know that in this job, nothing is as it seems," he reminds me of the first thing he told me.

"Yes," I smile.

So, I'm thinking to myself that this seems like reverse psychology. If Jesse Stanton is the obvious suspect, that probably means he didn't do it. Or, life doesn't work like that? I keep these thoughts to myself, wanting to remain professional.

"Just... be careful with the press, OK?" he urges me again. "They're like snakes. They can get you to say things you didn't even dream of saying, then wrap it up and make it look like you've just publicly admitted to killing the pope."

I chuckle at the thought. "Got it."

"OK then, you can get back to work, thank you," he dismisses me politely, focusing on the documents in his hand.

I smile, withdrawing from his office and go back to my desk. Once again, the card pops to mind. Dinner tonight, it said.

If he thinks I would ever have dinner with him, he's crazy. He's out of his mind.

Not only would it be wrong professionally, but also because of the fact that I dated his brother. Despite the fact that I don't feel anything for him anymore, it still feels wrong.

After another couple of minutes of going back and forth between this, I finally manage to get some work done. A few minutes after six, I realize that my working hours have ended. I switch off my laptop, heading down with the elevator. It's been a long day and I can't wait to go home, jump into a bath with nice, warm water and have a well-deserved glass of wine, forgetting all about Jesse Stanton.

Whether or not he did what he's being accused of is none of my business. That is, at least, what I keep telling myself, as I'm going down with the elevator. As soon as it opens, I walk out, greeting our security guard, Jonas.

"G'night, Miss. Watson," he tells me with the smile of a well-meaning grandfather.

To be honest, he's probably old enough to actually be my grandfather. They told me that he's been here with the building for forty years, and although there is little security he can provide, the whole building voted to keep him on the job until he retired. I thought that was one of the sweetest acts of kindness towards an employee I've ever seen. Acts like that remind me that there is still some goodness left in this world.

"I told you that you don't have to call me miss, Jonas," I smile at him. "Grace is fine."

"But that is what you are," he corrects me politely. "A lovely little miss. I can't imagine callin' you anythin' else."

I chuckle at his words. "Well, if that is how you feel, I don't mind then."

He nods, in the manner of an old, English gentleman who is seeing visitors away from his castle, leaving him behind, alone but not lonely.

"Good night, Jonas," I wave, as I leave the building.

A chilly summer breeze hits me immediately, and I pull my blazer tighter to my chest. I look around. The street looks busy. My bus will probably be late, as usual, so it'll take me an hour and a half to get home... as always.

At that moment, I see someone standing by a shiny, black car, leaning against it. He's looking at me. Something clenches inside of me, when suddenly, I realize who it is.

He's obviously expecting me to walk over there. Well... tough luck.

I turn around, and start walking in the opposite direction, pretending that I haven't seen him. It's a roundabout way, but I don't want to face him right now.

However, he doesn't give up.

"Grace!" I hear him shout.

I frown. He obviously doesn't refrain from shouting like that in the street.

I turn to him, shaking my head. He beckons me to come. I consider just turning around and walking away, but it's obvious that he needs to be put in his place first.

So, I do as he bids me. I walk over to him, standing right in front of him. Our eyes lock. The heavy scent of his cologne hits me like a tidal wave, but I don't falter.

"Why are you shouting in the street?" I ask, displeased.

"Well, what is a guy to do when he's being ignored?"

Chapter Four

Jesse

She really thought she'd get away with ignoring me.

I look at her, forcing her to hold my gaze. Her flaming hair cascades down her back, lifted up away from her face. She is wearing a dainty pair of pearl earrings, which stand in perfect contrast to her fiery locks.

"I wasn't ignoring you," she tries, but I don't let her.

"You can tell that to someone else," I grin. "But I'm not offended. Or better yet, I won't be, if you take me up on that offer."

"What offer?" she asks.

"Are you going to pretend you didn't get my flowers and that you didn't read the card?" I ask, feeling that I'm holding all the control in this situation. It makes me feel invincible, and it is going exactly according to my plan.

"I won't," she admits, tilting her head a little as she speaks. "But I also won't take you up on that."

"Why not?" I ask.

"I'm tired," she says. I have to admit, it sounds like the truth. "Also, I'm not dressed to go out."

"You look nice," I tell her.

Much better than nice, I think to myself, but I don't share that with her.

That dress is hugging her curves to perfection, although it is professional enough to allow everything to the imagination. As she was walking over to me, I couldn't take my eyes off of the way her hips swayed to the left, then to the right.

"Yeah," she frowns. "That's exactly what a girl wants to hear."

"OK, OK," I take it back a notch. "I think we got off on the wrong foot here."

"We've been on the wrong foot since we met," she reminds me.

Still, despite the fact that she sounds like a spitfire, I can see that the corner of her lips wants to spread into a smile. She's enjoying this as much as I am.

Taking into account what I know about her, I'm sure that this strategy won't work. So, I try another one.

"I know I came on too strong when I was here this morning," I start, trying to sound as apologetic as possible, exactly because I know she won't be expecting this of me. I continue in the same manner, and the surprise in her eyes is palpable. I have to admit I'm enjoying it greatly, seeing her like this.

"Allow me to take you out to dinner to make up for that," I finish my thought.

She looks at me somehow strangely, almost as if she's seeing me for the first time. Those green eyes are burning at me, and I wonder how come I didn't realize before how strikingly beautiful she is. Maybe because she was Bobby's girlfriend at the time? Or is it because she's blossomed into this girl I'm seeing before me now?

She sighs heavily, as if she has a very difficult choice to make. I also know what would tilt the scales towards my advantage, but I want to see whether I might convince her without it.

She doesn't say anything yet. I don't want her to refuse me again, so I take out the big guns.

"Please?" I say, with that look I've been told could melt glaciers.

It works exactly as I thought it would. She smiles. And it is the most radiant smile I've been given in ages. It mesmerizes me... but only for a moment. I immediately remind myself why I'm here. It's info. I can't allow myself to be mesmerized. That's for fools.

"You won't leave me alone until we do this, will you?" she asks, sounding defeated, but at the same time, playful. I'm all for it.

"You're absolutely right," I grin, stepping to the side of my car and opening the door for her.

"Oh, I didn't know you were a gentleman," she teases, getting inside.

I sit in the driver's seat and turn to her. "There are so many things you don't know about me... yet."

"Don't get ahead of yourself," she warns me, still not losing that playful tone. "Just because I allowed you to take me out doesn't mean I'll fall down to my knees before you."

I have to banish that thought from my mind the moment she says it out loud. Her, on her knees, before me... Mmmm. Delicious.

My cock springs to action immediately at the thought. Fortunately, my jeans are keeping it in place.

"I'm not expecting any such thing," I reply sweetly. "This is just a dinner."

But how long that dinner will last and where it will end is a whole different matter.

She doesn't say anything to that. Instead, she turns to the side and looks out the window. I focus on the road ahead of me, the traffic being a road through Hell itself, but eventually, we reach our destination. I park the car across the street from the restaurant, and get out first, opening the door for her again. She lets me, which I appreciate.

"We're here," I say, enjoying the look on her face when she realizes which restaurant I chose.

"Bella Italia?" she asks, gasping and turning to me. "But... that place takes reservations two months in advance!"

I swear, I never get tired of this. But also, I don't take all my dates here. These are for when I want to make an especially good first impression. Or in this case, fix it.

"Shall we?" I ask, offering her my hand.

She smiles so sweetly that I feel joy even in the forgotten recesses of my heart, the places I didn't even know still existed within me. The look on her face is that of a child being told that she can have anything she wants from her favorite candy store, even the most expensive candy. That sheer joy is such a rare, precious thing nowadays.

Again, I try not to think about it, as we're walking inside. I know all eyes are on us. They usually are, but especially now. I'm guessing the whole town knows the news by now. I can feel those glances burrowing into the back of my head. I can almost hear the whispers of disbelief.

When we reach the hostess, she grins at us immediately.

"Mr. Stanton," she greets me. "Always a pleasure. Your usual table?"

"Yes, please," I nod, doing my best to be as courteous as possible. The first impression I'm trying to repair here is horrible, so I have to do my best.

We are quickly seated at my usual table, and along the way, I nod to a few familiar faces. They smile back at me. I'm grateful that I don't see pity in their eyes. That's the last thing I want from anyone.

"So, did you have to sell your soul to the Devil to have a regular spot for you here?" she asks, giggling.

"Something like that," I grin back at her, enjoying the sound of her laughter far more than I thought I would. "I just– "

"Jesse!"

At that moment, I hear the voice of Filiberto Culotta, the proud owner of Bella Italia.

"Why, I knew it was you-a when I hear-a your voice-a!" Filiberto says with a thick Italian accent, even years after he had been living here. Still, that only seemed to add to the charm of this place.

I shake his hand cordially. "Always a pleasure, Filiberto," I smile.

"The same-a, the same-a," he nods. Then, he turns to Grace. "And this is your lovely date-a for tonight-a?"

"This is Grace Watson," I introduce her. "An old friend of mine."

"Oh, for an old friend-a we have to make-a something really special, eh?" He winks at me, and when I look at Grace, I notice she's really amused by all this. I just shrug helplessly.

"Surprise us, Filiberto," I ask. "You know that I rarely look at the menu here. I prefer your suggestions."

"I will not disappoint-a," he says again, patting me on the shoulder. He lifts his hand and gestures at the nearby waiter. "Cerretalto, 2016. Casanova di Neri." he says. The waiter just nods. Then, Filiberto turns to us again. "I have-a taken the liberty of ordering your-a wine-a. The food will come-a soon-a."

"Thank you," Grace suddenly voices herself, and he smiles at her.

"My pleasure, Miss. Grazia."

He bows before her, then retreats back to the kitchen.

"What a charmer, eh?" I ask. "How is a guy to compete with that?"

"No way," she giggles. "You have to be Italian. If you're not, it's game over."

"Is it now?" I laugh.

"Well, you've seen it yourself," she shrugs, playfully. "Smooth."

"Alright," I agree, unable to take my eyes off of her. "I can admit when I'm beaten."

"Can you?" she asks, teasing. "I didn't think that the famous Jesse Stanton had that word in his vocabulary."

"I didn't think so," I admit. "But now... I mean, he's Italian as Hell."

She laughs melodiously again, and a part of me suddenly wishes we were on a real date, and not just making it a means of finding out what her office knows regarding my case. Guilty conscience stings me, but I banish it from my mind. I have an agenda here, and I have to stay focused, otherwise everything I've worked for so hard all these years will be gone forever. Not to mention the fact that I might rot in jail for the rest of my life for a crime I didn't commit.

"Are you alright?" she suddenly asks, sounding worried.

"What?" I ask, and only then does my brain register her question. "Yes, yes. I'm fine. Sorry. It's this whole mess, but I don't want to talk about that right now."

"Oh," she says, looking confused. "I can't discuss that. I'm sorry."

I smile. "There's nothing to be sorry about. I would never put you in such a position, to jeopardize your job."

That is a damn shameful lie. I feel like a piece of shit saying every word of it, but that's how it has to be. She has to trust me. She has to want to help me. Whether or not she will forgive me for all this later is something else, something I'll worry about when the time comes.

"So, you bring all your dates here?" she suddenly wonders, as the waiter brings us our wine, pouring it first for her, then for me. I nod to him when he's done.

This is a trick question. I know it is. If I say no, she'll think I'm lying. So, I have to confirm, but carefully.

"I've brought a few of them here, yes," I admit. "But only because I like Filiberto's place that much."

She smiles.

Excellent, my wicked mind says. We dodged a bullet.

The food arrives immediately after, and Filiberto explains what it is.

"Bistecca Fiorentina for Jesse," he nods at me. "I know-a it is your favorite. And, for the lady..." he pauses as the dish is served, "ossobuco alla Milanese. I dare say-a that you have never tasted meat as tender as this-a!"

Upon those words, he kisses the tips of his fingers, and we all chuckle.

"Enjoy-a!" he says, bowing again, and returning to the kitchen, leaving us alone, although with those prying eyes still watching our every move.

Somehow, I've stopped caring. I watch Grace try her food, and she moans softly upon the first bite. I swear, I could kiss Filiberto just for that delectable sound alone.

"This is heavenly!" she says with her mouth full, covering her mouth with her hand. "Sorry..." she smiles, chewing quickly, then swallowing. "I just had to say that out loud."

"I'm glad you like it," I smile. "Filiberto will be happy as well."

The following two hours pass by in a whirlwind, and I realize that we've drunk the whole bottle, and finished not only our food, but also the dessert. I call the waiter for the bill, but he leans over to me and tells me it's been taken care of.

I glance in the direction of the kitchen, where Filiberto had appeared for one moment. He smiles, nodding. I bow my head gratefully, and once again, he disappears back into the kitchen.

"I would offer to drive you home, but I drank, so we'll call a taxi," I suggest.

"Thank you," she nods. "I like that you're being so careful."

We walk out to the sidewalk, and I hold her blazer for her so she can put it on.

She turns to me, with an odd look on her face. "You know, I never thought you were like this."

"Like what?" I wonder, really curious about her words.

"I don't know... nice," she says.

I chuckle. "Yeah... that's exactly what a guy wants to hear."

Her eyes widen in shock, then she bursts into a loud chuckle, remembering that these were the exact same words she told me when I said she looked nice.

"Come," I take her by the hand, without even thinking. "Our taxi is over there."

Chapter Five

Grace

Just one more drink.

That is what we agreed on in the taxi. I have no idea what came over me. But the truth was, I didn't want this night to end.

My body has almost forgotten what it feels like to have someone's hand on me, to have someone's lips on mine. And seeing Jesse this evening, having him behave the way he has been behaving all night has got me hornier than ever.

He unlocks the door to his apartment complex, which is on the top of a building. He allows me to enter first, and I gasp at his living room. The whole wall is made of glass, and it overlooks the entire city. I walk over there, gently caressing the curtain, which is pulled to the side. There are a million little flickers of light scattered about the city. It is so alive, just like me at this very moment.

That wine has really hit the spot, and I feel hot all over. I slide out of my blazer, and throw it carelessly onto the sofa, while I remain in front of the window, mesmerized by the sight before me. Underneath me, there is a thick, shaggy carpet, with my feet sinking right into it.

Suddenly, he walks up behind me, and slides his arms around my waist. He isn't wasting any time. Then again, I know why I came here.

A drink. Yeah, right.

Maybe if that's to drink in the sight of him on top of me.

"Did you ever make love with the lights of the city flickering right in front of you?" he murmurs into my neck seductively, and heat instantly pools between my thighs.

If anyone knows what they're doing, it's him. His lips slowly start kissing my neck, gently and tenderly, while his hands pull me closer to him. I feel his cock pressing against my buttocks, and while all logic tells me I shouldn't be here, all I can do is moan with pleasure.

I want this more than I thought I did. No. Even worse than that. I need this.

I would be lying if I said that I never imagined this moment. I would be lying if I said I didn't dream about this, literally. Then, I would wake up in a hot sweat, only to realize such a thing would never happen. But now it was.

"Mmm, you taste so good," he whispers again, and I feel his hands sliding down my thighs, pulling my dress up.

Then, he spins me around, and kisses me passionately, his tongue twirling around with mine. I can taste the wine we had, mixed with a faint scent of tobacco. I know he was smoking before. It used to bug me. But now, everything seems to be in perfect balance. Everything about him is pure bliss and I don't want to be caressed and cuddled. I want to be fucked by him. Hard.

I cup his face with my hands, gripping harder at him. I tug at his lower lip with my teeth, showing him how I want it. He pulls away to look at me, grinning in the darkness. Only the flickering lights are illuminating our silhouettes.

"You like it rough?" he asks. "What a nice surprise."

"There is nothing nice about tonight," I tell him.

"Fuck, Grace..." He groans, sliding his fingers into my hair and gripping it tightly, adjusting my neck, so he can kiss me deeply, wetly.

The moment our kiss is done, he lowers me onto the carpet, pulling off my tights, then taking my dress off. I do the same with his shirt, quickly unbuttoning him, while he's still kissing me.

It feels like we're in a rush, like we don't have enough time and we know it. But it's not the time. It is the sheer need, the raw desire that is taking over us both and there is nothing we can do to control it.

His lips are so soft. I bite at his lower lip again, tugging at it desperately. He pulls me closer to him, his arms around me, his skin on mine. I already feel so wet, my pussy is throbbing with need, and he hasn't even touched me yet properly.

"Wait..." he suddenly says, reaching to the side of the sofa, where a small nightstand rests. He extracts a condom from the drawer, and slides it onto his cock, which is already glistening from precum. I know he wants me as much as I want him.

"Lie down," I tell him. It is the wine talking. I would never talk to him like this. It is that stupid wine and I–

But he does exactly what I tell him.

"Do whatever you want to me," he tells me, and that is exactly what I plan on doing.

I stand over him, with my legs spread apart. I look at his eyes, then down his perfectly chiseled body, all in muscle, as if he were made solely of boulders chipped off of a mountain. Then, I drink in the sight of his need. His cock is standing up, thick and long, just waiting to be showered with attention.

I can't resist touching myself. I lower myself onto my knees, with my fingers gently spreading my pussy lips apart. I grind against his thick cock, and he groans with pleasure.

"Look at me," I tell him, and once again, he does exactly what I tell him, what the wine tells him.

I slowly sit down on his cock, feeling its fullness inside of me, all the way in, deeper and deeper.

"Oh," I moan loudly, closing my eyes, as I rest my hands on his chest, moving forward then backward. The feeling is exquisite. I keep grinding against him, keeping eye contact as I do so. I am already so close, my body fueled by good wine, good food and a man with a cock to die for.

I keep fucking him slowly, making him enjoy every single thrust as much as I am enjoying it. Then, I hasten the pace, pressing my clit against his lower belly. He reaches his arms towards me, his fingers caressing my pebbled nipples, pinching them, teasing them. The sensation is too much, and I cum instantly, without thinking, without expecting to.

Heat explodes inside of me, from the very depths of my being, and the warmth spreads throughout my entire body, filling me with bliss. My pussy clenches around his cock still inside of me, but I don't stop moving. I keep grinding through the ecstasy, and when he feels my body relax, he grabs me, making me lie down this time.

He adjusts himself between my legs, putting them on his shoulders, sliding his cock into me again gently, with my climax lubricating the way.

"Oh, Jesse!" I shout loudly, my mind obliterated by the angle which he's hitting in this position.

"Do you like it?" he asks, staring at me, his eyes wild and dark, and my hair spilling all around me.

"I love it," I admit, biting my lower lip, and he keeps fucking me again towards the brink of madness.

It's dirty, and wonderful at the same time, the way we're fucking each other like animals, not taking our eyes off of each other, demanding all our attention. My pussy juices are leaking out, as he effortlessly slides into me, fucking me to oblivion. Once again, he manages to make me cum, with my heartbeat all the way down in my pussy, throbbing and clenching, and all I can do is let go and completely lose control of myself.

A moment later, he follows, his body tightening, pumping hard once, twice, thrice. His cock pulsates inside of me, swelling and leaking.

Instead of pulling out immediately, he lowers his head to kiss me on the lips softly, almost lovingly, which I wasn't expecting. Then, a few moments later, he rolls off me, lying down onto the shag carpet, which I realize only now is more comfortable than I expected it to be.

I don't know if it's the wine or some general fatigue, but I fall asleep immediately. I have no idea how long I've been in that position, when I finally open my eyes again. I look at the window. It's still dark. All I know is that I have to go home. I can't be here in the morning when he wakes up.

I slowly get up, grabbing all my clothes and putting them back on in the hallway. The key is in the keyhole. I turn it as gently as I can, trying to make very little noise. The door finally opens, and I slide out of the apartment, running towards the elevator and pressing that button like crazy.

A few moments later, I'm out of the building, the night watchman just nods at me in passing, so I do the same. As soon as the chilly night air hits me, I feel like all that madness evaporates out of me, and I can finally think straight.

"Oh, my God..." I whisper to myself, inhaling deeply, staring at the empty street.

I can't believe that I did that. All that. It's not like me at all.

It's the wine. It has to be that wine. Two glasses and I was drunk, behaving like a wild girl, something I've never been. But somehow, I can't help but think that it was partly him. He awakened something inside of me, something I didn't even know I had, and the wine just helped bring it out to the surface.

I see a taxi in the distance, so I step on the curb, raising my hand. He sees me and stops. I huddle inside.

"Long night?" a man slightly older than me, with a thick beard and glasses asks me, looking at me in the rearview mirror.

"You don't know the half of it," I admit, proceeding to tell him my home address, and that's where we head immediately.

Fortunately, the guy is talkative for the both of us, so all I need to do is nod. The truth is I'm barely listening to him. I'm still wondering what will happen tomorrow.

But as soon as my head hits the softness of my pillow, I know I'll think about that tomorrow. For the time being, I am still under the impression. I know this was just a one time thing. I can't allow this to happen again. I just can't. Too much would be at stake.

I fall asleep with those exact thoughts on my mind, thinking it's the end, while in fact, this is only the beginning of the wildest ride of my life.

Chapter Six

Jesse

When I wake up in the morning, she's not there.

Usually, I have to force the women to go home somehow, because they conveniently become way too comfortable, helping themselves to coffee and breakfast. To be honest, I thought this would happen with Grace as well, and seeing her gone without even as much as a goodbye, really surprises me. Shocks me, even.

I walk over to the kitchen. Nothing. She probably got up in the middle of the night and without making any noise, sneaked out. I chuckle at the thought. I probably should have expected it of her, but instead, I thought she was just like all the others. Maybe that's my first mistake.

I grab my cell and dial her number, which I had my guy dig out for me. It rings several times. It's a workday, so she should be awake and at work. Maybe that's why she's not picking up?

Yeah, that's probably it. Otherwise, she would.

That's what I keep telling myself, because it hasn't happened yet that a girl didn't pick up when I called her. Usually, I don't even need to call. But with her, it's different. It has to be even more smooth than usual, because I'm not doing this to marry her or even date her long term. I need to clear my name, and she is a sure ticket for that.

Suddenly, I remember last night. Little snippets of what she did, how she acted, what she said, all of it rushes back to me like an avalanche. That's out of some sexy fairy tale every guy dreams of. Something tells me there is more to this, more to who she is and with my brother, she was just half of herself. She did not let go.

Pride roars in me, thinking I managed to open her up, at least up to a certain point. Curiosity surges through me, thinking what else she might be hiding. It seems that on this quest to prove my innocence, I might actually get to have some fun as well.

Just as I was thinking of sending another batch of flowers to her office, I hear the door buzzer. I frown. Usually, the security guard would let me know someone's coming up. Him failing to do so this time doesn't sit well. I'll have to see who's on duty today and sort it out.

I walk over to the door, reluctant to talk to anyone, but the moment I open the door, I recognize them immediately. I mean, I don't know their names, but I can see who they are. Cops. A woman and a man, always conveniently set up to play good cop, bad cop. Usually, the girl is the good cop, but in this case, I'm not sure if I'd bet on it.

Her hair is short, almost inmate-length. Her jaw is square. Her stare is dead serious. There is not a single feminine trait on her face.

"Mr. Stanton?" she speaks first. Her voice is womanly, but still stern, almost like an authoritative teacher who only knows how to give detention and F's.

"Yes," I nod. "And you are?"

"I'm Detective Sanchez," she shows me her badge, which she pulls away before I can take a look at anything on it and put it to memory. "This is my partner, Detective Williams."

The other guy does the same. His features are softer, but I'd bet he can pack a punch himself, if made to do so. His uniform is slightly wrinkled, and there is a small stain on his sleeve. Spilled coffee in a rush?

So, he must be the good cop then. The clumsy one. The one you'd expect to understand you if you asked him to.

Then, they both look at me expectantly.

I sigh. "Would you like to come in?"

It's best to play along. I'm probably not their favorite person right now, so I'd best not muddy the waters any more than they already are.

They don't reply, and instead, I step to the side allowing them in. They walk through the small hallway and into the living room, which in my mind, still smells of sex. Feeling guilty, I walk over to the window and open it.

"We know you've already spoken to our colleagues down at the fifth precinct," Detective Williams tells me. "We just wanted to come here and clarify a few things."

"Sure," I shrug.

A psychologist friend of mine once told me: if you are not guilty, do not be nervous or stressed. Those things make you look guilty as hell. I always took that as good advice. So, especially in a situation such as this one, staying level-headed seems like the best thing I could do.

Although, I'd much rather tell them to go to hell, to be honest, asking me the same fucking questions ten times, as if they didn't record the fucking interview and haven't written down the crucial things. Morons.

"How can I help?" I say instead, fighting my own thoughts.

Detective Williams withdraws a small notepad from his pocket and starts flipping through the pages, until he finally finds what he's looking for.

"You said that on the night of the 27th, you were home," he asks for clarification purposes.

"Yes, I was here," I gesture at the apartment.

"Can anyone corroborate that?" he asks.

"I already answered that," I explain. "The night watchman, Philip, saw me come home around nine, maybe a little before that."

"Yes," he nods, writing something down. "And you remained here for the rest of the night?"

"Yes," I nod again, clenching my teeth.

Why ask these stupid questions again? I don't get it.

He flips through a few more pages, then continues. "When was the last time you were there?"

"I don't know," I shrug, feeling a sudden need for another cigarette, but I've made it a rule not to smoke here. A rule I'm very close to breaking right now. "Maybe earlier this year? I honestly don't remember. It's just a weekend villa. When I'm swamped with work, I don't go there for months."

"Who takes care of the place?" This time, Detective Sanchez asks.

I turn to her. "No one," I reply. "When there's no one, the place is locked up. If we want to go there, I call a cleaning agency, they send someone over immediately, they clean up and we're good to go. I don't have anyone who goes there regularly to check up on the place."

Detective Sanchez frowns at me. "Aren't you afraid someone might break in?"

"I pay the security agency for that," I explain. "Besides, I don't have anything of value there."

"What about the TV? The sound system? The paintings?" she asks again.

"Oh, those," I say dismissively. "That's just furnishings. I meant, I don't keep any money there, jewelry, safes or stuff like that."

"I see," she nods, but something tells me I didn't convince her of whatever she wanted to be convinced.

"What about the parties?" Detective Williams asked.

"What parties?" I ask without even thinking. A moment later, it hits me. Of course, I know what parties he's referring to.

"Well, I don't know how you refer to them," he answers. "The parties you held there, with lots of VIP's."

"Ah," I nod, scratching the back of my head. "Well.. everyone throws parties now and then. Is that a crime?"

"It's a crime when someone ends up dead," Detective Sanchez seems to have been waiting for something like this to come up, so she was ready with a bomb.

I look at her. "But that girl didn't die during one of my parties. Besides, I didn't organize them. It was my brother and his best friend.

I attended sometimes. Other times, not. But they... I guess, needed my name so famous people would come."

"I see," she says again in that same way that is starting to piss me off, but I know I can't say anything. "Do you know when was the last time your brother, Robert and his friend...?"

"Shawn," I tell her.

"Shawn," she repeats. "Do you know when they were last there?"

"I don't know," I say again, sounding like a broken record at this point, but it's the truth. "I'm not their keeper."

She grimaces at me. "You let them go there whenever they feel like?"

"Bobby is my brother," I shrug. "Why wouldn't I let him go there?"

She doesn't say anything to that. She turns to her colleague, giving him a meaningful glance.

"Do they have a key?"

I swallow heavily. This is where I need to clear Bobby's name, although I know he's had nothing to do with this. He still has the keys, but he always tells me when he's going there and when they want to throw one of their parties. He hasn't told me about anything lately, so I'm assuming nothing's been taking place there.

"Bobby had a key, but he gave it back to me," I tell them.

It's a lie, but a necessary one.

"I see."

I swear, if I hear those words again... I try to calm down as Detective Williams scribbles down something else in his notepad, then closes it. I can only imagine that it means we're done. At least for the time being.

"Thank you for your time," Detective Williams tells me, sounding even polite.

"Sure thing," I nod, walking with them back to the front door. "Like I told your colleagues yesterday, I will do my best to help find out who did this."

Detective Williams suddenly offers me his hand. "We really appreciate it, Mr. Stanton."

"Of course," I nod, squeezing it back.

I glance at Detective Sanchez, but she has no intention of shaking my hand. That's fine. I'd rather they were gone as soon as possible anyway.

"If you remember anything that might help our investigation," he adds while they're still at the door, "please let us know."

"I will," I nod, actually liking the guy.

I close the door a moment later, wondering when the end to this will come. I know they're probably watching my every step. The fact that one detective was nice doesn't mean shit. I'm their number one suspect, and I know they're just waiting for me to slip up, so they can prove that I was there and that I killed that girl, a girl I didn't even know.

I inhale deeply, that desire for a cigarette stronger than ever. First, I find out that money is somehow leaking out of the company, and now this. I feel like someone's out to get me, but who?

Chapter Seven

G race

Don't pick up.

Don't call him back.

Forget all this ever happened.

Those are the thoughts repeating in my mind over and over again. While the Romero case has always taken precedence over anything else, my boss is still doing his best not to neglect the other active cases. That means that our morning has been hectic, with me dealing with the press, just like he predicted, without having any time for a lunch break.

Fortunately, that also meant that I haven't been able to focus much on Jesse and what happened last night. He tried calling me once in the morning, probably when he got up and noticed I wasn't there. Hopefully, he got the hint. If he didn't, I'll just have to explain it nicely when I see him that it was a mistake that can't happen again.

When I finally have the time for a bathroom break, I return to find another bouquet on my desk. It's not sunflowers this time, but rather a strangely wonderful combination of marigolds, carnations and zinnias, all orange in color, with just a little bit of greenery thrown in there, for good measure.

At that moment, my boss comes out of his office, closing the door behind him.

"I'm out for the day, Grace," he tells me. "I won't be returning."

"All right, Mr. Jennings," I nod dutifully.

His eyes fall on the flowers. "A wonderful bouquet. A thoughtful boyfriend?" he smiles.

We're not that close to discuss personal things, but I can tell that he seems to like the flowers, and that the question was purely out courtesy.

"Just a friend," I smile back.

"Those flowers say he wants to become something more," he chuckles. Then, before I can say anything to that, he waves at me heading for the elevators. "See you tomorrow, Grace. Don't stay too late now."

"I won't," I promise, still smiling.

A few moments later, I'm left alone with the flowers, and I don't even have to check who they're from. The card says exactly the same thing as yesterday. I decide to leave the flowers in the common kitchen on the second floor. That way, no one will know who the flowers are for or from. And everyone will enjoy them.

As for the card and the offer, I know what he will do. He'll be waiting for me in front of the building, but I'll outsmart him. I'll use the fire exit.

The following two hours pass relatively quickly. I try to focus on work, but I keep thinking about his offer.

Maybe one more time? Just one?

I have to admit, it does sound tempting. And what is the difference between doing something once or twice, and then stopping? My body immediately heats up at the memory of the previous night, and I know that if we end up alone somewhere, I might succumb to his charms again.

So, no wine tonight. No dinners. I'm going straight home.

That sounds like a great plan... in theory. Let's see if I'll be able to put it into practice.

I check the time. I still have about fifteen minutes until the end of my workday, but I know Mr. Jennings won't mind if I head on home a little earlier. This way, I'm sure I'll avoid Jesse, and I'll also avoid getting into trouble by sleeping with him again.

I know that if Mr. Jennings finds out, it might create trouble for me. In fact, it might create trouble for him as well, and that's the last thing I want to do. I could have excused myself last night somehow, that we've known each other for a long time, which is true, and we stumbled onto each other. Blah, blah, blah. Those sort of silly explanations people give when they want to do something they're not supposed to, and they don't really care whether someone will believe them or not.

However, I want to keep this job, and despite what happened last night, I'm taking it very seriously. Mr. Jennings trusts me. I don't want to lose that.

I slide out through the fire exit, and I run for my bus. Fortunately, it's on time. Everything seems to be going my way tonight, leading me home as quickly as possible. I know that once I'm home, I'm safe. Jesse can't get to me. I'll just switch off my phone and spend the night relaxing before I go to bed.

I ride the bus for about half an hour, before I finally reach my street. I jump off, continuing to walk towards my apartment complex. I say hello to a few neighbors, and a few minutes later, I'm locking the doors to my apartment, exhaling with relief.

"Not tonight," I smile to myself.

Right then, I hear a familiar meowing sound from the kitchen, and she peers a moment later from the doorway.

"Titi," I smile at her. "How are you, sweetheart?"

I walk over to her and pet her. She closes her eyes, lifting her head in a satisfied way, adjusting herself to my hand.

"Let's feed you first," I say. "And then everything else."

She meows again in agreement. I pour some food into her bowl and watch her eat for a few seconds. The other bowl is filled with granulated food, but my princess Nefertiti prefers it juicy. And meaty.

"Ok then," I tell her, "I need a peaceful night. Can we agree on that?"

She doesn't say anything. "I'll take that as a yes," I chuckle.

I go to my bedroom, opening my wardrobe and picking out a comfortable, oversized t-shirt to wear, after I get out of the bathroom.

The first thing I do is pour myself a glass of wine. Then, I light up a few candles, and run a bath, pouring in some bath salts and I even add bubbles. The kid in me loves them beyond description.

I watch the bath get filled with water and foam. I inhale with pleasure. All that aroma of strawberry and bubblegum in the air is enough to make you forget about all your troubles.

I take off my t-shirt first, then my pants. Just as I'm about to take off my underwear, someone rings the doorbell.

"Are you freaking kidding me?" I whine to myself.

Titi meows in the hallway. I peer at her, pressing my finger to my lips.

"Titi!" I shout, whispering at the same time. I never knew how difficult this is to do until the moment I had to try it. "Shhhh!"

But instead of listening to me, she meows again, prantzing over to the door and scratching it gently. That immediately makes whoever is on the other end of the door ring again. Longer this time. That assures me that I won't get away with pretending I'm not home.

I sigh heavily, grabbing my robe and wrapping myself in it. I take a peek through the keyhole, half-expecting to see Jesse of all people. But it's not him. It's that annoying lady who lives below me.

I open the door, mentally preparing for the endless conversation that is about to follow.

"Mrs. Wesley," I smile at her. "Good evening."

"Grace, my dear," she says theatrically, as the actress that she used to be, only she seems to forget that she is nearly eighty now, and that too much make up makes her look like a clown, which definitely isn't the look she is going for. However, no one has the strength to tell her that. "I've been waiting for you all day."

"You have?" I frown. "Why?"

"My nephew is in town," she tells me, lifting her eyebrows as she speaks, hinting at God knows what. Actually, I do know what she's hinting at. I just pretend not to, because I don't want to go out with her nephew, something she's mentioned several times now, and also something I've said no to an equal amount of times.

"Oh, that is very nice," I say, choosing my words. "But I'm afraid I'm too busy. Work, and... and my mom is coming for a visit."

That's a blatant lie, but she doesn't know that. Then again, I could make it true. Maybe mom could come and visit. I feel like I haven't seen her in ages, and I miss her terribly.

"Why, that is wonderful!" she claps her hands again as if she were the audience this time, and I were the actress. "Then all four of us could go out for dinner, or some nice show."

"Yeah," I say, clicking my lips together, and using my left hand to tighten my robe, in an effort to indirectly show her that I was sort of in the middle of something. But people like that never take subtle hints. You have to be direct with them. Only, you can't be direct with a lonely old lady who means well.

"I don't really know when exactly she'll be coming, so I can't promise you anything," I try to get out of this. "Maybe your nephew won't be here anymore and again, I don't want to make promises I can't keep."

"How about I give him your number and he can call you?" she suggests persistently, smiling through those unevenly rouged lips, and herself tightening her own silk bathrobe, adorned with Chinoiseries motives, like swans, leaves and blossoms. All she's missing is ostrich feathers around her neck, I think to myself.

"I have an idea," I suddenly tell her reassuringly. "Why don't you give me his number and when I have the time, I'll call him to arrange something?"

"All right," she beams at me, so overjoyed that I feel bad this was a lie. "I'll bring you that number immediately.

"You make sure to do that, Mrs. Wesley," I tell her, grinning, at the same time hoping she will just fall asleep in front of the TV as she always does and forget about all this.

She waves as she heads back towards the staircase, and I do the same, proceeding to close the door. When I turn around, Titi is sitting right behind me, giving me the look.

"What?" I ask, shrugging. "You heard her. She wants to set me up with her nephew who's thirty and still unemployed. Are you kidding me?"

I expect her to meow in agreement, but she doesn't. "Traitor," I stick out my tongue at her, passing her by and heading towards the bathroom.

I still have a chance of enjoying a nice, relaxing evening, despite this interruption. If she rings again, I'll just pretend I've fallen asleep in front of the TV or something. I'll bring her some store-bought cookies tomorrow as an excuse and that'll be that.

I take off my robe and then my underwear, slipping into the velvety softness of the bubbly water. The heat washes over me instantly, relaxing all my muscles at once and untensing me.

I turn to my left side. My wine glass is there, next to my phone, which is playing some soothing music.

"Ah," I murmur to myself. "You deserve this..."

I make small waves with my hands, enjoying the peaceful sound. Occasionally, Titi walks in because I always leave the door ajar. She doesn't like it when she can't reach me. It's been like this ever since I found her, about half a year ago, out in the cold. She was wet and shivering in a cardboard box by the dumpsters. Someone must have left her there to die.

I heard her meows, and I couldn't just turn away. I brought her up to my apartment, fed her, warmed her up and just... kept her. My landlord has no idea she's here. I'm guessing it'll probably be a problem if he does eventually find out, but as always, I'll cross that bridge when I get to it.

For now, Titi is here with me and she's not going anywhere. She's learned that I have to go away, but she's also learned that I will always come back. Still, when I'm home, she likes me to be available at all times. That is why there are no closed doors and I'm OK with that. We both are.

She meows suddenly, bringing me back to the present moment. She is standing on the other end of the bathtub. It hasn't happened yet that she fell in, but I'm guessing she might.

"Be careful," I smile at her. "You know you hate getting wet."

Sometimes, I feel like she really understands me. She takes a step back and jumps down from the bathtub, walking out of the bathroom. I smile to myself, shaking my head.

I slide deeper under water, closing my eyes. This evening is pure perfection. I can't imagine anything ruining it.

Chapter Eight

Jesse

"I think she left," the security guard tells me.

"Can you check?" I ask. "It's important."

He looks at me just once, and reconsiders asking me why.

"Sure," he nods instead, walking over to his desk and picking up the phone. He dials a number, and after a few seconds, he hangs up.

"There's no answer," he tells me.

"Are you sure?" I ask, but one look in his direction provides me with a silent reply.

"Yeah," he nods. "No one's picking up. They must have all gone home already."

"OK," I nod, turning around and walking back to my car.

There, I sit wondering why she has to be stubborn and refuse my advances. Any other girl would be glad to be in her shoes. Any other girl would be running after me, as they usually do. Maybe she knows why I'm doing all this?

I frown to myself. There is no way. I haven't told her about this. I will just keep convincing her that it's all because I'm sorry I treated her so... badly. Although I haven't really done anything wrong. I didn't tell Bobby to break up with her. I just told him I thought she was a gold digger.

I guess I wasn't thinking. If I had spoken to her on occasion, I would have realized that she is nothing like that. She works hard. I can tell immediately. She's smart and doesn't rely on others to do things for her. I guess these are all things I wasn't paying much attention to when I was advising Bobby. But that's all in the past. You can't change any of the shitty things you did. You can only affect the here and the now.

For a moment, I consider just leaving her be. She obviously doesn't want to pick up. She doesn't want to see me. I should respect her wishes.

But I immediately remember what's at stake here. I'm being accused of something I haven't done, something that puts me at risk of losing everything that I've worked for so hard. I can't allow that to happen. Grace can help me find out what they have on me, what evidence and can I find a way to exonerate myself from this shitstorm somehow.

I try calling her again, for the third time, but the result is the same. I hang up the phone, continuing to check through it for her address. When I find it, I set the GPS coordinates, and head there immediately. I reach her apartment complex, parking a little down the street.

Just as I'm about to press the button for her apartment, the door opens, and a lady looks at me.

"Visiting?" she asks, a little more directly than I like, but I bite my tongue, because she opened the door for me.

She's actually made it easier for me to get to Grace. Ringing her buzzer from downstairs could mean that she might not even let me into the building, let alone into her apartment. But if I knock on her door, there is less chance of her slamming it in my face once she realizes it's me.

"Yes," I say, trying to walk past her, but instead of going her way, she starts climbing up with me, trying to keep up.

"I don't usually go to throw out the trash this late," she says without being provoked into speaking. "Old ladies like me are an easy target, you know."

She says it with the theatrics of a damsel in distress, only she is not a damsel nor is she in distress. She is merely one of those nosey old ladies who has nothing better to do than check up on her neighbors constantly.

"You're right," I tell her, urging her then to follow her own advice, as we're climbing up the stairs.

"I haven't seen you here before," she points out.

No shit.

Only, I have more manners than to say this out loud.

"You're right," I choose to say instead, hastening my step. Surprisingly, she does the same.

Then, I stop in front of the door I know is Grace's. I turn around, and surprisingly, she is standing behind me still, just looking at me.

"You're here to... see Grace?" she asks, tilting her head in a strange way, as if to take a closer look at me, to size me up. I almost chuckle at this, but I manage to remain serious. Obviously, this lady isn't right in the head.

"Yes," I nod, about to turn around and knock on the door, when I hear her voice again.

"Are you two dating?" she asks.

My eyebrows knit, and I have to swallow my surprise at her audacity.

"I don't mean to sound rude, lady," I say, amused as well as shocked, "but what's it to you?"

She straightens her back a little as she speaks, adding to the caricaturized image that she is already projecting. She rests her hands on her hips. Her lips pout only slightly, revealing uneven lines of her lipstick, that no woman her age ought to be wearing for the simple fact that it screams at whoever is looking at her. I try to keep my eyes above those two frightful lines, but it's difficult.

"Well, if you want to know, she is dating my nephew," she tells me importantly.

"Your nephew?" I repeat, wondering who the hell she is and even more, who the hell is her nephew.

"Yes," she affirms. "So, if you are here to ask her out, you should just... turn around and go back where you came from."

As soon as she says those words, she gestures at me with her hands, as if I'm a bird that has flown onto her field and it is now eating her grains. The whole situation is beyond ridiculous, and I have to focus all of my conscious effort not to burst into laughter.

"Don't worry," I tell her, realizing that this is the only way to get her to go home and leave me alone. "I'm not here to take her out."

I'm here so she can tell me everything she knows about my case. But I cleverly keep this to myself.

"Oh," she says, sounding a little startled now. "Well... that's good. Because my nephew really likes her, and I want this to work out for them. They make such a sweet couple."

I grin. "I believe you."

I look at her expectantly, wondering if this is where our conversation ends, or will she tell me more about her nephew. Despite all common sense, I've gotten invested into this little drama. I can't remember the last time someone amused me to such an extent.

"I'm here for a work related reason, lady," I tell her. "I'm not trying to steal your nephew's girlfriend."

"Well, that's a relief," she says, with a smile this time. "I'm glad to see that there are still decent young men out there, who will not try to steal another man's woman. Back in my day, this didn't happen as often as it happens nowadays."

"I'm sure it didn't," I stifle a chuckle. I give her another meaningful glance, but I realize she has no intention of letting me be. "If that's all, Mrs...?"

"Mrs. Wesley," she informs me because I asked. "I live in the apartment below."

She says it in a way that assures me she would stay up all night if necessary, just to assure herself that I will leave and that nothing will happen. Only, I can't vouch for that. I am here for a purpose. For two, actually. The thing is that one leads to another.

Again, I get that little pang of a guilty conscience, something I haven't been paying much attention to lately, I'll admit. However, I can't allow my guilty conscience to wash over me now. Not like I'm hurting her in any way. I just want to take her out a few times, woo her, see what she knows. She'll get pleasure out of it as well. I'm just not being all that honest with her.

But that's the world we live in. You can't promise anyone anything, because what is true today might not be true tomorrow. And there is nothing you can do about it. Not like you can control your feelings. You love someone today, but can you vow to love them until you die? No. That's impossible. It defies logic.

All we have is here and now. All we have is the present moment. And all we can do is make the best of it. People are being unrealistic about this I'll love you til the day I die crap.

At that moment, I realize that this lady won't go away until she sees me walk into Grace's apartment. Then, she'll probably stay glued to the peephole, waiting for me to come out and go home.

I smile at her, turning to press the doorbell. It's a soft sound, with two notes. I'm wondering if she'll check who it is.

Mrs. Wesley and I are having our own little private staring contest, when finally, I hear the key turn from the other side, and Grace's voice echoes the moment she opens the door.

"Mrs. Wesley, you didn't need to bring me the number now," she starts, but she stops the moment she realizes it's me and not the annoying lady from downstairs.

"Jesse?" she gasps, gripping at the towel, with her fingers, as tiny little droplets of water are still dripping down her naked skin.

Then, a moment later, she realizes I'm not alone. "Mrs. Wesley!?"

Her eyes dart from her to me, then to her again. I decide to take over, although this is becoming more and more amusing.

"Hey Grace, I came to bring you that... thing... for that... case, we talked about earlier," I tell her, again stifling a chuckle.

"Yes, that... thing," she gestures at me, nodding. "And Mrs. Wesley, I'm sorry, but we'll talk tomorrow, if that's alright with you."

It was obvious that it wasn't alright with her. But Grace had no intention of apologizing for anything, although the lady seemed shocked to see me, then her open the door in a towel, as if she was expecting me for a night of passionate love making. I have to say I love that idea.

"Good night, Mrs. Wesley," I say as well, just before Grace closes the door.

Our eyes lock, and I can see she's frowning.

"I don't know why you're here, but don't think I won't throw you out the moment you piss me off," she tells me, and all I can do is burst into a loud chuckle, the same one I've been holding in all this time.

Chapter Nine

Grace

"You know why I'm here," he finally says, once he stops laughing.

I know I'm in my towel, which basically means I'm naked. Well... in a way. He can't see anything, but someone being in a towel evokes images. Naughty images.

"No," I reply stubbornly.

"You didn't respond to my offer for dinner tonight," he reminds me of something I don't need to be reminded.

"Isn't silence enough of an answer?" I wonder.

"You know I don't take no for an answer that easily," he grins at me, and for some reason, I grip at the towel even more firmly. I can't imagine a more awkward situation than if my towel somehow dropped right now. Knowing how clumsy I am, I wouldn't be surprised.

I shake my head at him. "This is all just a game to you, isn't it?"

His grin disappears, which surprises me. He turns serious. "No. Why would you think that?"

"You don't care at all whether you'll get me in trouble with my boss," I continue, feeling frustrated first with Mrs. Wesley, for not being able to tell her that I'm really not interested in dating her thirty year old unemployed nephew, and secondly with Jesse, who is in my apartment, without being invited.

"Grace, I really don't want to get you in trouble," he admits.

His voice is slow and calm. He isn't grinning. He isn't smiling. He is as serious as I am, and for some reason, I trust him. Although I don't want to.

"You just being here means I could get in trouble," I remind him. "You know where I work. You've been there. And yet, you come here, pushing for us to... I don't even know what. What do you want from me?"

"Well, first, I would like you to calm down," he says softly. "Can you do that?"

"No, I– " I start, but at that moment, Titi walks out of the bedroom.

She isn't used to strangers, and she usually just shies away in the bedroom when I'm having guests, even when my mom is here. But this time, it's different. Titi comes out on her own. She seems a bit apprehensive, but a moment later, she heads straight for Jesse, rubbing herself against his trouser leg. I'm looking at this and I can't believe that I'm seeing it. The traitor.

"Well, hello there," he immediately shifts his focus to Titi, going down to one knee. The little feline traitor is acting even worse now. She is allowing him to cuddle her, even purring. "What is your name?" he asks as if she might actually tell him.

"Titi," I say, although I didn't mean to.

"Titi?" he lifts his head to look at me.

"Yeah, from Nefertiti?" I explain, not expecting him to know.

"Akhenaten's wife," he nods.

My eyes widen in shock and disbelief. He seems to like it.

"You're not the only one who likes to read up on Ancient Egypt," he explains, getting up, which Titi doesn't like one bit. She remains around his legs, much to my surprise.

"The beautiful one has come," he adds, referring to the translation of Nefertiti's name into English.

"OK, OK," I pretend not to be amazed. "You don't have to flaunt your knowledge of Ancient Egypt here."

He smiles. It isn't a grin, but a sweet smile. A real one. The kind he rarely bestows on anyone.

"Not that I don't like looking at you like that," he says, pointing at my towel, "but maybe you'll feel more comfortable dressed."

"Oh," I look down at my body.

He's right.

My cheeks blush fervently, probably matching the color of my hair. I rush back to my bedroom and grab my oversized t-shirt, the one I sleep in. It hides most of my body, so it's a good, quick choice. When I return, I find him on the sofa with Titi in his lap, dozing off.

"Seriously?" I ask, shaking my head, unable to hide my amusement.

"What?" he wonders.

"I can't believe this," I gesture at her. "She never does this. With anyone."

"I feel honored then," he chuckles, scratching her neck, which she extends to give him easier access.

I inhale deeply, walking over to the armchair opposite the sofa where he's sitting with Titi in his lap. Then, I sit down myself.

"Do you want to tell me now why you're here?" I ask. "We had sex. You don't have to pretend like you want something more with me. I know what that was, and it's OK. I'm not heartbroken or anything, so all this..." I gesture at him, "is not necessary."

He wasn't expecting to hear that. I can see it in his facial expression. Wow. I must be the first girl who did this to him. Well... good.

"Besides, we can't be seen together," I add, although I doubt he doesn't know this. "You're a suspect. And my boss is helping gather the evidence against– "

At that moment, it hits me. I gasp silently. My jaw drops.

"That's it, isn't it?" I ask, incredulously.

"Grace, just hear me out, OK?" he says, getting up and tenderly moving Titi out of his lap, onto the sofa. Then, he walks over to me. "I wasn't expecting to see you at the office when I went there. And yes, it occurred to me to maybe see what you know, what your boss knows, but I haven't asked you anything, have I?"

I hesitate to reply, as if this might be a trick question. "No."

"I mean, I wanted to," he admits. "But… I know it's not right."

The following question just pops out of me, like a sudden explosion, without either of us expecting it to happen.

"Did you do it?" I ask.

The moment I ask him, I know it was a stupid question. I already know the answer. But I need to hear him say it.

"Are you really asking me that?" he sounds as incredulous as I am. He shakes his head at me. "I thought you knew me. I thought you knew me at least well enough to know that I would never do something like that. I've done many shitty things in my life, but taking someone's life…" He shakes his head at me again but doesn't continue.

Instead, he turns away from me and starts heading towards the door. Without thinking, I rush after him, grabbing him by the elbow. That makes him stop. He turns to me again. He's not angry. He's not afraid. He seems… broken somehow. I don't know if anyone is that good at pretending.

"I just want to find out the truth," he tells me, without waiting for me to apologize. I guess an apology doesn't even matter. My actions spoke louder than my words.

"That's what I want as well," I tell him. "That's what my boss is after."

"But you know that sometimes, people like me are a target," he reminds me.

"I know," I nod.

"That's why I wanted to be close to you initially, to see where the investigation was going, so I could do some investigating of my own if it starts heading in the wrong direction," he admits.

He walks over to the sofa again and sits down. As if she were waiting for him, Titi climbs into his lap again. He smiles at her, petting her head tenderly. Then, he looks up at me. Those eyes are burning straight through me, and I know he's telling the truth.

"When I found out what happened, I... I was stunned," he continues. "I didn't know what to do at first. The police questioned me in a way that assured me it's just a matter of time before they connect to me to it, other than her being found on my property. I don't know what happened. I really don't. If I did, I would be at the police station, telling them everything. But I don't. I don't know anything that might shed light on that poor girl's murder. So now, this whole thing is breathing down my neck, and I know the cops aren't looking for anyone else."

He pauses, to let that sink in. But I know what he means. We exchange a meaningful glance, and then, he continues. "I know they are trying to pin this on me, and they're basically looking for clues to close this case as soon as possible, making the most obvious suspect, which is me, the one responsible."

I try to find some reassuring words, but I know he's right. It wouldn't be the first time something like this has happened. Although it is frightening to even consider it, there are people in prison who have been wrongfully convicted of a crime. If they are lucky, after a few years spent behind bars, they manage to prove their innocence. Some never get the chance to do so. I shudder to think that this might be Jesse's fate.

"I just want to find out the truth," he tells me, sounding defeated. "I know that means putting your job at risk, so after I leave here, know that you won't have to deal with me again. But to clarify... I wasn't intending on playing any games with you. What happened last night... I wanted it as much as you did, and it had nothing to do with that murder."

I frown. "I don't like having murder and sex with me in the same sentence."

I try it out as a joke. He smiles, although weakly.

He pats Titi again, pensively. She stirs in her half-sleep but doesn't move.

I realize that maybe he's not such a bad guy as I thought he was. This side of him I'm seeing now is new. I didn't even know he had it in him. This vulnerable side, a side that can open up so much.

"I also want to find out the truth," I tell him. "And... I think that the truth is more important than anything."

I don't know if this is stupid of me, but I can't stay away from all this. I thought he was just playing me, but it turns out he is just like the rest of us, afraid for his own well-being. He isn't immune to this human fear. And he, more so than the rest of us now, has enough reason to be afraid.

I have to help him, even if that means jeopardizing my job.

"I'm glad you think that," he smiles, much more convincingly this time. "But it was wrong of me to put you in this situation."

"No, no," I shake my head at him. "I think... I would have probably done the same thing."

He looks at me puzzlingly. "You would?"

"Mhm," I nod. "I mean, I can't even begin to understand how you feel, but if that happened to me, I would also use any possible means of finding definite proof that it couldn't have been me."

"The only definite proof is to find out who did it," he tells me.

"Exactly," I agree. "That's why I will help you."

His eyes widen at me, almost as if he's seeing me for the first time, really seeing me. Then, his lips widen into a smile I've never seen before.

"You will?" he asks, incredulously.

"Of course," I assure him. "We should all have the same goal and that is the truth."

That is, in a way, correct. Although, I'm stretching it.

I know why I'm doing this. I want to help him. I didn't want to admit this to myself, but I like having him around, especially now after seeing that he isn't the jerk that I thought him to be.

Suddenly, he moves Titi from his lap. She looks up at him, surprised that he dared to move her. She stretches her grey, stripped legs, then struts out of the living room, giving us some privacy.

He stands up to face me. "You're the last person I thought would help me," he whispers, taking my hand into his.

Immediately, a surge of electricity courses through my body. I know where this will lead. I know and I welcome it.

He doesn't say anything else. He doesn't have to. He can see exactly what is written in my eyes. My own desire mirrors his.

He leans over to me slowly. I could stop him at any moment, but I don't. I want this to happen as much as he does. Our lips lock and he does it gently, tenderly, wrapping his arms around my waist and pulling me closer.

Chapter Ten

Jesse

There are a million little voices inside my mind, competing with each, trying to be louder than the other one, as I'm kissing her wildly, completely letting go.

I hear so many things.

Stop.

Don't stop.

Take her.

Don't take her.

Fuck her.

Don't fuck her.

Love her.

But there is no negative to this one.

She moans into my lips, and my cock springs inside my pants. Something deep inside of me is urging me to go on, although that heavy feeling of a guilty conscience is still here, fucking up the moment. I need to erase all these doubts from my mind. I try to banish all thoughts, good and bad. I want an empty mind. I want to be in the moment with her, to Hell with everything and everyone else.

She shivers as I pull her closer. I push her against the wall, lifting her arms above her head.

"You are so delicious," I murmur against her neck, inhaling her scent. "I want to eat you alive."

My other hand slides down her curves, behind her back to her ass, grabbing as much of it as I can into my palm. I unbutton her blouse, pulling down her bra just a little, exposing her pebbled nipples. I can't resist them. I take one of them into my mouth, sucking it, teasing it. She closes her eyes, moaning, biting her lower lip. I don't know how I never noticed this before, but everything about her is so exquisite.

I gently tug at her nipple, leaving it wet with saliva. I move on to the other one, as my hand slides down her milky white stomach, unbuttoning her pants. She shudders under my touch. Her arms are still above her head. Her entire body stretched out, waiting to be touched. I want her completely at my mercy.

"I want you to cry with pleasure," I tell her, flicking my tongue over her nipple, as my fingers slide into her panties.

I use my knee to spread her legs apart. My finger parts her wet folds, stopping at the very entrance. She moans loudly, opening her eyes.

"Is that what you want?" I ask.

"Mhm..." That is all she manages to say.

I grin in the dark. "Tell me."

"I want you," she says.

"To do what, baby?" I love it when good girls speak naughty. It turns me on so badly.

"I..." she starts, biting her lower lip, and I flick my finger over her pussy slowly, tantalizingly, so she can feel the buildup.

"You what, baby?" I ask again, my nose caressing her neck.

Fuck, she smells good.

"I want you..." she says again, her voice so fucking hot.

"To?" I urge her, licking her earlobe, down to her collar bone.

"To fuck me..." she finally says it.

"Good girl," I grin against her fragrant skin, sliding two fingers inside of her.

"Oh..." she moans softly, arching her back against the wall, spreading her legs even wider for me, allowing me better access.

We both hear that wet noise. I know when I slide into her, it's gonna be amazing. But I want to prolong this moment a little longer.

"You're so wet for me..."

Saying those words out loud does something to us both. I slide my fingers out of her, then back inside. She is on fire. Her entire body shivers, as I fuck her with my fingers. Our lips lock.

"Open your eyes and look at me," I demand.

She does it immediately. Her eyes are wild and dark, as if a wild animal is staring at me from behind them. I keep fucking her, my thumb finding her clit easily and rubbing it. The combination of those two sends her over the edge. I see that moment in her eyes, the moment she lets go. Her pussy clenches around my fingers, then releases. She moans loudly, her lips pressed to mine. She clenches again, several times, enjoying the slow release.

I slowly pull my fingers out of her. They're dripping with her juices. I bring them to my mouth and suck on them. She tastes so fucking good.

"Do you want me inside you?" I ask, completely taking over control this time.

I wanted to be more gentle that first time, but now, I can't. I want her so badly. I want to own every part of her being, to make her mine, to make her forget about every guy before me and every guy that might come after me. Tonight, she is mine.

I take her by the hand and lead her to the sofa. I sit down first. She doesn't need to be told anything. She steps over my legs, taking my cock into her hands. It is throbbing, beading with precum. I'm desperate for release. But I want to wait as long as I can. The very sight of her warm, wet pussy is enough to send me over the edge.

She doesn't look away even for a single moment. She is much bolder now than before. Her fingers around my needy cock feel amazing. She is gentle at first, squeezing it harder with each grip. Then, she brings her pussy closer to it, pressing just the tip to her entrance. She is playing, rubbing it along the seam. I want her to sit down on it. I want to feel her heat envelop me, but she is taking her sweet time, torturing me.

Finally, she lowers herself onto it. She bites her lower lip as she welcomes me inside. I feel like her pussy is melting onto my cock, wet and hot. She doesn't sit all the way down, but instead, brings her ass up.

"Fuck..." I groan loudly, unable to hold it in.

She sits down again, more slowly this time, more deeply as well. Her ass grinds against my shaft. I grab hold of her hips. Her tits are in my face, perky and white, teasing me to lick them. But I can't take my eyes off of her beautiful face. The look of pleasure is etched in those eyes, on those lips. Seeing how much she wants this only turns me on even more and I can't look away.

I grip at her waist, as she starts to thrust and slide, grinding against me. I let her have all the control. She takes me in so deeply that I'm sure she can feel every inch of me, throbbing desperately inside of her.

She keeps moving, following her own rhythm, as I slide my fingers down and find her swollen clit. She immediately starts moving faster. Her gyrations become more and more frenzied. Her back is arched. Her breasts are on full display, bouncing as she moves. They are pure perfection. The look on her face as she throws her head back is nothing short of pure ecstasy. I've never seen a woman like that, in the throes of passion, completely having surrendered to the moment.

I couldn't even believe that she would let go so easily, to such an extent. Looking at her as she is now, she is the sexiest woman alive. No other could ever touch her. No other has ever made my cock throb with such a need to burst.

I take control at that moment, slamming into her. I start rubbing her clit faster and faster.

"Oh, fuck, Jesse!" she screams, and I know she's close, just like me.

Maybe we could prolong this for a few moments more. I want this explosion. I want to come completely undone with her.

Her hair falls down her back like a fiery waterfall. I entangle my fingers into it, pulling her head even more to the back, exposing her tits. I open my mouth, swallowing one nipple whole. My cock pulsates violently.

At that moment, her body shakes and I know she came again. I feel her pussy clenching around my cock, drawing me in. The feeling is amazing. I never want it to stop. Her juices ooze out of her, onto my balls, wetting them.

I expect her to keep fucking me, but instead, she rises up and falls down to her knees before me. My cock is in her hands. I'm so swollen, ready to blow up. She squeezes it, controlling my release.

She opens her mouth, offering her tongue to me. That is the moment all control goes to Hell. I explode at the sight of her sparkling, pink tongue before my cock. My hot seed sprays her lips, her cheeks, her mouth. It takes me a few seconds to completely drain myself.

Still breathing heavily, I watch her smile. She goes over her lips with the tip of her thumb, wiping them off. Then, she climbs up onto me and gives me a peck on the cheek.

She gets up, walking about the room, which is half-illuminated. In the darkness, she looks like a femme fatale from some old fifties, noir movie. All she's missing is a small handgun and she'd be perfect.

But she is perfect, as she is now. That thought forms inside of me so naturally that it takes me off guard. I can't think that. I have to focus on what matters. I have to clear my name, otherwise everything that I've worked so hard for will be lost.

"You don't have to go home, you know," she suddenly says, standing in the doorway. "It's OK if you sleep over. That doesn't have to mean anything."

She doesn't wait for me to reply. I listen to the sound of her footsteps disappearing somewhere down the hall. I have two choices now. I can go home, just like she did, or I can stay.

It doesn't take me long to make my choice.

I get up from the sofa, my cock still dripping. My body is still in ecstasy, but it's slowly releasing its grip on me. I follow her to the bedroom. Everything is in a dreamlike state. She is in bed, her back turned to me. Titi is down where her feet are, unbothered.

For a moment, I wonder how it would be to do this every night for the rest of my life. The thought doesn't seem half bad.

I slide into the bed, under the covers and I press my body against hers. I listen to the soft, rhythmical sound of her breathing. Maybe she's just pretending to be asleep, maybe not. It doesn't really matter. There is nothing else left to say, at least not for the time being. Our bodies have said it all.

I welcome the sound of silence and I drift off to sleep.

Chapter Eleven

Grace

I open my eyes to an empty place in the bed next to me. For a moment, I feel sad, as if a rope suddenly tightened around my heart, but it lets go immediately, as soon as I remind myself that I should have expected it. All those words were just something he said to get me in bed again. And I fell for it.

I frown into the pillow. I meant every word I said last night about the truth, about everything. But I guess he–

At that very moment, my racing thoughts are interrupted by noise in the kitchen. The clinking of pans. The opening of the cupboards.

I prop myself up in bed. Titi is on the floor. I only now realize she's there. She looks up at me with those big eyes, probably wondering the same thing I am.

Is he still here?

I'm not sure if I said this aloud or did this question remain inside the confines of my mind. I guess it doesn't matter. I jump out of bed, realizing that I'm still naked. I grab my oversized t-shirt, the same one from last night, slip into it, then head to the kitchen.

Much to my surprise, he is there, fiddling with the coffee machine. He's with his back turned to me. I don't think he's heard me come in.

Titi walks into the kitchen a moment later. She meows loudly, and this is the noise that makes him turn around.

"Oh!" he grins.

He's wearing just a pair of boxer shorts, which tighten around his hips. His bulge fills the entire front part, and I try not to look in that direction, so I quickly look up at him, wondering if he noticed me staring at his manhood.

"Good morning," he says.

"Morning," I reply, walking around the kitchen island and over to him. "Need any help?"

"I think so," he says, looking confused.

He rakes his fingers through his dark hair, and instantly, the memory of what happened last night, hits me like a hurricane. I blush at the amount of desire that washes over me. I've never felt such chemistry with anyone.

"Why don't you go sit down?" I suggest. "I'll make us a coffee, and something to eat."

"I could help," he offers.

I smile. "Just sit down and relax. It'll take a minute."

He does as he's told. Titi, of course, immediately starts circling his legs and he bends down to pet her, which was what she expected.

"You ran away," he reminds me. "I didn't."

I'm reaching for the coffee from the upper left cupboard when he says this. I stop for just one moment, then I continue. I don't turn around, because I know I'll get even more confused if I have to look at him while I'm explaining myself.

"I didn't run away," I say, putting the ground coffee into the coffee machine which clicks familiarly into place, once I've adjusted the big spoon. I press the button, and a moment later, a buzzing noise is heard, preventing me from speaking. It buys me about half a minute before the noise stops, and I know he's expecting me to continue.

"I had work in the morning," I explain vaguely. "I had to go home, take a shower, get ready for work." I turn around, feeling like I've got this under control at this point. "I can't go to work in the same clothes as the previous day. What would that look like?"

"Like you slept at someone else's place, which you as an adult, are allowed to do?" he teases.

The moment our eyes lock, I lose all that confidence that this is under control. Nothing is under control. Him being here, now, wanting coffee and breakfast, after a night of lovemaking, means that nothing is under control. Under my control, anyway.

"You know it looks unprofessional," I shrug, pressing the button for another coffee, and a few moments later, serving them both on the table.

"I actually thought you were a gold digger," he says, catching me off guard.

I mean, I knew this, but I didn't know he would mention it now.

"And you're surprised I'm not?" I ask him playfully, taking a seat opposite him.

"My mistake was in not giving you a chance," he says again, blowing my mind with his statements. "I assumed, and you should never assume."

"People can surprise you," I smile.

"Exactly," he nods. "I guess, when you're in my position, you expect people to only want to take advantage of you, in any way they can."

He pauses, allowing these words to sink in. I ponder on them. He's right.

"I can't imagine how difficult it must be for you," I tease, although it is all lighthearted. "To have all that money, to be able to do whatever the heck you want. Oh, poor you." I smile while I'm speaking, so he can immediately tell that I don't mean it seriously. At least, not all of it.

He smiles back. Those pearly whites flash like the brightest stars in the night sky. I take a moment to appreciate the symmetry of his facial features. His square jaw, his chin, his well-proportioned nose. Everything about him looks like it has been equally measured. Only his Adonis-like body is too... handsome. That just isn't fair.

"Money can buy you many things," he replies. "It can even buy health, in the sense that you can get all the best medicine, all the best treatments in any hospital, with any doctor in any country of the world."

"Well, that is all you really need, isn't it?" I wonder, taking a sip of my coffee.

Never, in a million years did I think I would be sitting with Jesse Stanton in my kitchen and drinking coffee with him, after a night of passionate lovemaking. If someone ever suggested that to me, I would call them absolutely insane.

"In a way," he agrees, taking his cup and bringing it to his lips. He takes a small sip, then puts it back down. "But it can't make people like you. Actually, like you and be your friend. It seems the more money you have, the more people envy you, the more they want to see you go down, and they will go so far as to pretend to like you, and then stab you in the back like it's nothing."

I listen to him speak, and I realize that there is so much to him I didn't know. I guess we both made the same mistake about assuming things about the other one. I assumed he was a jerk who just wanted to take advantage of girls and just make them into another tick on his list in his little black book. He thought I was a gold digger. I guess we were both wrong.

"It must be difficult living like that, not knowing who your real friends are," I agree.

He shrugs. "You get used to it. After a while, you become very careful about who you let in. The same goes for your family. When you were with Bobby, I... I couldn't understand why."

I frown. "You couldn't understand what?"

"Why you were with him," he admits. "I mean, you're way out of his league. He's my brother and all, but facts speak for themselves."

"That's not very nice of you," I say. He probably meant it as a compliment, but I didn't see it as such. "Bobby is a nice guy. I like nice guys."

"Of course," he nods, pressing his lips together. He looks apologetic now. "I should have known that before I jumped to conclusions. I just thought you liked him because he was related to me, and you know..."

I'm still frowning. I'm not enjoying this conversation very much, but it's more genuine than many of the conversations we had back when I was dating Bobby.

"Not everything revolves around you," I remind him. "Me dating your brother had nothing to do with you."

"I believe you," he says. "And I didn't mean any disrespect. I just sometimes don't think about the words I'm saying. Forgive me?"

He looks at me in a way that makes it impossible for me to say no. I smile back at him.

"There's nothing to forgive," I shrug. "I like that we're... clearing the air, so to speak."

And actually, I do. I want to know more about him. I want to be reassured again and again that he isn't the jerk I always thought him to be. I want to see the guy from last night, the guy from this morning, although I know he can't always be this person.

I jump up from my seat. "Eggs?"

"For breakfast?" he asks.

"Yes," I chuckle. "Unless you mean to stay here for lunch as well."

Immediately upon saying that, I bite my tongue. I don't want him to think it's an invitation. At the same time, I don't want him to think that I wouldn't like that.

Ugh. I have no idea what is the exact message I want to convey right now. It's blurry inside my mind, and he's the reason for it.

"Breakfast is fine," he eyes me mischievously. "Then, I have to get going. It's the weekend, but when you own a company that makes billions a year, you never get a day off."

I can't help but think how much he likes to repeat that. Then again, he is the one responsible for making that company blossom into what it is now. No one helped him. He didn't inherit it from his parents. He started off as a poor nobody, and now, everyone knows his name. If that isn't something to be proud of, then I don't know what is.

Still, I like guys who are more modest. Nice. He's neither modest nor that nice, but sometimes, I catch a glimpse of the person he might be hiding. Maybe he had to become who he is now, because of that wealth. Money changes you. Sometimes, not for the better.

I ready the eggs, expecting him to talk more, but he doesn't. When I occasionally turn around, as if to grab something, I see him petting Titi, who is enjoying it greatly.

"I honestly can't believe she's behaving like that with you," I can't hold my tongue about this, because it's not only surprising, but also downright shocking.

"Dogs like everyone," he points out. "They're just like that. It's in their nature to be trustworthy and to think the best of everyone. But not cats."

When he says this, he scratches Titi behind the ears and she meows softly, stretching her front paws all the way ahead of her.

"Titi isn't trusting at all," I point out. "Even with some of my friends who've been coming here for months."

He smiles. "Don't. You'll make me blush."

I chuckle at his comment. "It wasn't meant to make you blush, just pointing out something I'm shocked by."

"If a cat likes you, then she's seen through you," he tells me. "We had a cat when we were kids, Bobby and me. She got run over by a car."

"Oh, I'm sorry to hear that," I say, almost gasping.

"It's OK," he shrugs. "Shit happens. But while she was with us, she was the sweetest thing ever. Loved my mom. Loved Bobby and me. Hated the rest of the world. It didn't matter if you were Mother Theresa, she hated you all the same."

"I wouldn't call her sweet then," I smile, hoping that I didn't cross the line.

"With us, she was," he corrects me. "And then, she was gone. Bobby wasn't affected at all, I guess because he spent the least time with her. But Luna, that was her name, she followed me around everywhere."

He pauses here, reminiscing. I can see it in his eyes. For a moment, I'm sure that he wasn't petting Titi. It was Luna's soft fur underneath his fingers.

I'm brought back to the present moment by the sound of crackling oil and eggs.

"Oh, oh!" I turn, taking the pan off the stove, and serving the eggs into a plate. One for Titi, of course.

A minute later, I'm seated opposite him at the table again, and the situation feels even more cozy than before. I don't know how safe it is to open up to him. I don't know if I should be doing this, but how can something that feels so right, be wrong?

This is what I'm thinking as we're both eating in silence, exchanging coy glances every once in a while. My heart is awakened, but not in a way that makes me yearn for his presence at all times. It's just a state of wanting to know more, all there is about him, to be away from him so I can miss him. It's a strange, conflicting sensation that won't let me be and I know that it might eventually get me into trouble.

But I'll cross that bridge when I get to it.

Chapter Twelve

Jesse

I'm a dirtbag.

It's as simple as that. There is no other way of saying this.

I told her all the things she wanted to hear, all the things she needed to hear so she would be on my side.

I grip at the steering wheel to my car, burying my face into it. No matter how tightly I close my eyes, Grace's face is still in front of me, through the darkened haze of stars in the darkness.

It was so easy to tell her what she wanted to hear. Words just kept pouring out of me, in a flood. I couldn't have stopped them even if I wanted to. Only, I didn't. I still don't. I want her by my side, but strangely enough, I'm starting to enjoy her company more than I thought I would.

My main goal is still to prove myself innocent in all this, and I know that she will do her best to help me. That has been my goal. And I'm well on my way. Then, why do I feel like an asshole?

At that moment, my phone rings and I quickly pick up.

"Yeah?" I answer when I realize it's my brother.

"Jesse?" he asks, as if it wouldn't be me picking up my phone.

"What is it, Bobby?" I ask, and the moment he says my name, I know something's wrong. I know he's worried. And the situation is such that if he's worried, I'm also.

"The cops were just here," he tells me. "They asked me... questions and I... I didn't know... I said things... I..." He starts stuttering as always when he's upset and apprehensive, so I do my best to calm him down.

"Just breathe, Bobby," I remind him. "Relax."

"All right, Jesse," he replies on the other end of the line. He says it, but I know he's far from calm.

"Where are you?"

"At home," he tells me, in the same tone of voice.

"OK, stay there," I instruct. "I'll be there in half an hour."

"OK," he replies. "See you soon."

I hang up the phone, inhaling deeply.

Shit.

I knew they would hone in on him. They could see from the first moment of questioning me that I won't go down that easily. Hell, I refuse to go down for something I didn't do. So, now, the cops know they have to go the roundabout way, which has always been Bobby.

Just like I promised, I arrive at his place in half an hour. I can see from the moment he opens the door that he's still worried, even more worried than I am.

I walk in, closing the door behind me.

"Coffee?" he offers.

I shake my head. "I have to get to the office, so I won't be staying long. Tell me what happened."

He sits on the sofa. I don't know if I'm imagining things, but he looks like he's aged about ten years in the past ten days. Out of the two of us, he's always been the one to worry more. It's as if he's always been clever enough to see that there's a problem, but rarely clever enough to come up with a solution. I know it's not the nicest thing to say about your brother, but when you come to a certain age, you just can't keep turning a blind eye to certain things.

"They questioned me about the parties," he starts. "I said Shawn and I didn't host any in ages."

"And you told the truth," I nod. "Why are you worried then?"

He looks at me as he did when we were kids. Those blue eyes and once blond hair that has gotten darker now always got people's sympathy, unlike me. Not that I minded. It taught me that I had to fight for respect. Otherwise, I would get sympathy. Honestly, I would always take respect over sympathy. As for Bobby, he's the kind of person who's always fine with whatever you give him. Even now, I'm sometimes surprised how different we are, although we are brothers and the same mother raised us.

I won't even mention our dirtbag of a father who left her when she was pregnant with Bobby, and never spoke to her again. Didn't even come to her funeral, motherfucker. But he had the balls to come to my office and ask for money. I told him never to contact me again. He still tries, sometimes. But always gets the same reply.

"I'm worried you might go to prison," he admits, just like he did when we were kids, when mom was working two jobs to keep our little family afloat, and I had to take care of him.

I walk over and sit on the sofa next to him. "This is a shitty situation I'm in, that's true. It's obvious that someone is trying to pin this on me, but luckily, so far I've managed to evade becoming an official suspect. I probably have a little more time to prove my innocence, and I have to use it wisely."

I immediately think of Grace and how I'm using her selfishly, putting her at risk. She's my direct connection with Jennings and his findings. I have to know what he knows. But at the same time, I have to keep her under the impression that it's not just that.

To be honest, my mind is a mess. My heart has been locked up for a very long time. Opening it isn't an option. I know I'm a lying scumbag, but at least, I'll be a lying scumbag who won't spend the rest of his life behind bars. That's something. I'll give some money to charity and that should make me even.

But what about Grace? I hear that little voice ask.

I don't know what about her. It's more than just sex with her. Or maybe, it's just my guilty conscience trying not to make me feel as guilty as I already feel.

Whatever it is, I can't get entangled in anything right now. I have to focus on keeping my ass out of prison, like I've been doing all this time. I did do a few things on the way to the top, some things I'm not proud of, some things which might land me with huge fines, but at least, I've never done anything worthy of being sent to prison. I promised myself that would be where I draw the line. Besides, you can't get to where I am in life without cracking some eggs along the way to make that omelet.

"Don't worry, OK?" I try to reassure him. "You just tell me if the cops start harassing you and I'll deal with it. It's one thing to ask questions for an ongoing investigation, and it's something else harassing someone."

"No, no, they didn't," he tells me, shaking his head. "I just... I'm always afraid I'll say the wrong thing."

"You can't say the wrong thing if you say the truth, always remember that," I remind him.

I pat him on the back, then I get up. He does the same. He's a bit shorter than me, so he's always slightly looking upward when our eyes meet. He's always been skinnier, smaller. That has always made him a target. And mom spoiled him. Well, as much as she could under the circumstances. That isn't a good combination. Protecting him has always been something I did without even thinking about it. If you mess with my brother, you mess with me. It was as simple as that, and the boys at school where we went soon learned that... the hard way.

"I'm dealing with this, OK?" I tell him again, just in case he needs to hear it one more time.

"Tell me if there's anything I can do," he offers.

I smile. "I appreciate it," I nod. "But I can handle it on my own. When I find out who is trying to frame me, I promise you they'll wish the cops got hold of them before I did."

I leave Bobby's place feeling strangely that the clock is ticking even faster than usual. Maybe Bobby's concern rubbed off onto me, and now

I can't shake it. I don't like it. I need a clear mind. I need to focus on what I need to do.

I drive to the office. The building is empty, apart from a few employees who still have enough willpower to want to prove themselves. I head to the top floor, relishing the solitude of my office. I open the window, which overlooks the entire city. I always loved this view. It makes me feel like I own this city. I guess in a way, I do. Only these past couple of days made me feel like that isn't true anymore.

This city has become my enemy. Somewhere in there, hiding in those streets is someone who killed an innocent girl, all so they could frame me for the murder. The thought fills me with rage. I feel sorry for the girl, but I feel even more sorry for whoever did it, because when I find them, I won't have any mercy.

I walk over to my desk and take a seat, opening my laptop. I asked for access to our financial records in the past four months, but I doubt anything will be shown here, apart from some unnecessary expenses.

After half an hour of staring at the numbers, it is just as I thought. I can't find anything wrong, yet the money keeps flowing out of the company, much more than usual.

I sigh heavily, rubbing the bridge of my nose. There is a leak in my company. I just know it. However, I can't seem to pinpoint who is the person or the persons responsible.

At that very moment, my phone rings and I grab it, thinking it's Bobby. I frown at the unknown number displayed on the screen.

"Yes?" I reply.

"Jesse?" The deep, husky voice from the other side says, and I immediately recognize it. He is the last person I want to talk to right now.

"I told you to fuck off," I remind him, a second away from hanging up on him.

"Just hear me out," he starts. "I don't need it for booze. There is this business opportunity, you see, and if we both invest, I guarantee– "

I can't listen to him right now. I hang up, taking my phone and smashing it against the wall opposite me. It explodes as it hits the wall, falling down onto the carpet into a million little pieces.

My whole body is tense, as if I've swallowed poison, and now it is coursing through my veins, with me unable to do anything about it but endure the pain. My jaw tightens at the thought that the man who made me only calls to get money from me, but he didn't give two shits whether we had something to eat or not.

I know I can't stay here. These walls are suffocating me.

I get up and head out of the office and straight down the hallway towards the elevators. I have no idea where I'm going. The only thing I do know is that I can't stay here.

Chapter Thirteen

Grace

It's silly of me. I know. It's silly, stupid, and totally unlike me, but I can't help but expect him to call or send a message.

The whole Saturday goes by. Nothing. Then the whole Sunday.

On Monday, I try to remind myself that it's ridiculous to be this invested in something, in someone, but I can't help it. I want to be there for him. I want to find out the truth with him, and I want to be there when this whole thing blows over. I want him to know that I helped.

I know how ridiculous it all sounds. I know everything, but my heart refuses to listen to any reason. That is the sort of determination I walk into my office building that Monday morning. I still haven't heard from him, but that doesn't change anything.

I make myself comfortable at my desk, and about fifteen minutes later, my boss walks out of the elevator, heading for his office.

"Good morning, Grace," he greets me on the way.

"Good morning, Mr. Jennings," I smile back.

"Any calls yet?" he asks.

"No," I shake my head. He nods, then disappears inside his office.

I fidget on my chair for a few minutes, realizing that I want to go in and ask him about Jesse's case, but I don't want to make it too obvious. Maybe I could wait for another reason to go into his office and then just steer the conversation in that direction.

An hour passes and I can barely focus on work. There are phone calls, but I'm doing it all without even thinking about it. My mind is elsewhere. When I hang up the phone, I realize I can't have the whole day pass by like this. I take the notes from the phone calls, and I muster all of my confidence to knock on his door. He immediately calls me in.

"There were three phone calls," I start, although none of them are urgent or even important. Still, they are my ticket in and I'll use them. "The first lady asked about our working hours."

He frowns. "Working hours?"

"I know," I nod, shrugging. "I told her and that was that." I look down at my notes. "The second call was about a case from last year, the Bakersville trial, but I said we don't give out information about current or previous cases." He just nods to this, without saying anything. "Finally, the third one was your daughter who said she'd be stopping by later, because I said you'll be here all day."

"Thank you, Grace," he says politely.

I realize that, if I don't say anything, he will dismiss me, and I won't have another chance to start this conversation. It's silly really, because we often talk about cases, especially ongoing ones. I don't know why everything seems so different with this one.

Perhaps because everything is different. I've never been personally involved in a case. Not like this, at least. And I feel like I have to walk on eggshells, otherwise something terrible will happen. I dare not think in that direction. I want to remain in the present moment, when I am standing by Jesse's side, and he can rely on me for help. That is the reality I want to be in.

"How is the Romero case going?" I ask, trying to sound as casual as I can.

He lifts his head from his desk. His glasses slide down his nose slightly, so he pushes them back with his index finger. They are thick, Coke bottle thick. I wonder if he even sees anything without them.

"It's pretty cut and dry," he tells me without any hesitation.

That's not a good thing. Our cases usually aren't cut and dry.

"What do you mean?" I ask.

"The billionaire did it," he shrugs.

"He did?" I gasp, but then I remember that I'm not supposed to sound like I care at all. Only, that's easier said than done. So, I clear my throat a little before continuing. "I mean, The body was just found on his property, but it is known that he doesn't live there."

"That still doesn't mean that the place is abandoned," he corrects me. "He's admitted to going there often, having parties there."

"They weren't his parties." It's my turn to correct him on this one.

He lifts his eyebrow at me and gives me a knowledgeable glance. He's trying to read me. I can tell. All I can do is remain calm and composed, but my heart is beating like crazy.

"He can't prove anything," he finally continues, without focusing on me at all, for which I'm grateful. He's good at reading people. I don't want him to read what I feel about Jesse, mostly because I'm still not ready to admit it myself.

"It's his house, but he doesn't go there often. The parties took place there, but he didn't attend. The people who attended them were not his friends, but his brother's? I mean, seriously." He tilts his head as if to take a better look at me, and I know exactly what he is thinking.

To be honest, I know how this sounds, especially when he puts it like this.

"So, you're sure it's him?" I ask again.

"I'm not sure of anything," he replies. "I'm simply following the evidence, as always. And right now, all evidence points in the direction of Jesse Stanton."

"Of course," I nod.

"It's a headache of a case," he adds, rolling his eyes. "The publicity is enormous, and the DA is breathing down my neck."

"I know," I agree. "The press keeps calling about it nonstop."

"You have to make sure that nothing leaks out of this office, Grace," he tells me in a conspiratorial manner, as if it's the two of us against everyone else.

I immediately feel a pang of guilty conscience. He just told me that I need to keep the press under control, while it's actually me who's socializing with the person I'm not supposed to.

Once again, I try to make sense of it all. I should either keep away from Jesse or at least tell my boss to keep me in the dark about it. But I can't do either of those two things. I need this job. I need to prove to my boss that I'm a hard worker who deserves to stay here indefinitely, because that's what my plan has become. I can see myself working here for many years to come, and I hope to get more promotions. However, in order to make that come true, I need to prove myself.

How the heck can I prove myself when I'm doing exactly the opposite of what is expected of me?

But at the same time, I can't keep away from Jesse. Something is pulling me to him, and I realize that all that aggression that we'd been harboring between us while I was dating his brother was simply sexual tension in disguise. I never would have guessed so, but having made love to him proves it. It's like I opened a door, and now, I'm unable to close it.

Not only that, but there is the issue of truth. Jesse is right. On his way up, he must have made several enemies, even those he did not see as enemies. When you are successful, envy is all around you. There are many people who want to see you fall down, to see you ruined. I'm sure that this is exactly what's happening here. Someone is trying to frame him, and we have to find out who that someone is, before it's too late.

Obviously, my boss is led by evidence as always. However, in this case, the evidence is pointing in the wrong direction, because someone has made it appear that way.

"You can count on me, Mr. Jennings," I tell him, nodding.

In a way, I didn't lie to him. Of course, he can count on me. But he can count on me to find out the truth. Now more so than ever, it is of the utmost importance that I keep helping Jesse, even if that costs me more than I intended to invest in all of this.

"I know that Grace," he smiles at me. "You keep that up and there's a bright future for you here."

His words mean more to me than I could ever express. I smile back at him.

"Thank you," I reply. "Well, I won't keep you any longer…"

"Just one more thing," he says before I can reach the door. "Can you get Williams on the phone and tell him I'll come to see him an hour later? I just can't make it on time."

He looks around his desk helplessly. It's a mess of papers, one on top of the other, an endless row with folders, sticky notes and arrows pointing in all directions. I wonder how he can work in such a mess. Usually, it's not like this, but obviously, this case has got us all entangled, even someone who is very pedantic, like Mr. Jennings.

"Of course," I nod, heading out of the door.

As soon as I sit at my desk, I do as my boss told me. I call Mr. Williams on the phone and reschedule their meeting for an hour later. He doesn't seem that upset and ends our conversation by wishing me a nice day. I do the same.

The following several hours pass by unusually quickly. The press keeps calling again, and just like my boss instructed me, I keep giving them nothing. But this is their job. They want the story, and they'll do anything to get it. That is why we need to be extra careful, not only here, but also when we go out together.

I realize that can't happen anymore. If Jesse and I are to continue… seeing each other or whatever else we're doing right now, that has to happen in secret. That means no more dinners, no more outings. Nothing. That way, we are keeping a low profile, and only that way can we continue to work together in finding the truth.

However, I have to tell him what Mr. Jennings revealed. That means that we don't have as much time as we thought we did.

When I'm done with work, I head home, but not to stay.

"I just came back to feed you, Titi," I tell her, but she pays little attention to my words, as she stuffs her annoyingly cute face into the food bowl, making satisfied cat noises. Her tail swings left and right, as usual, when she's eating.

I watch her for a few moments, wondering if it's a good idea to go. But these doubts are quickly dispersed from my mind, and instead of them, Jesse's face illuminates the dark confusion reigning inside of me.

I'm falling for him. Hard. And it's obvious. I can't even pretend that I'm trying to fight it. I'm letting go, like Alice falling down the rabbit hole, and I have no idea how deep it goes. All I know is that I want to keep falling down with him, no matter where I end up eventually.

A moment later, I head towards the door. Only when I open it again does Titi lift her head. The noise pulled her out of that food related focus. Our eyes meet. I smile.

"I'll be back quickly, OK?" I tell her, absolutely sure that she knows exactly where I'm going.

Before she can meow a reply back, I close the door, locking it and I head downstairs, where a taxi is already waiting for me.

Chapter Fourteen

Jesse

I have another drink, but it does little to alleviate the stress. If I didn't know any better, I'd think it's making it worse.

I pace about the apartment like a caged tiger, wondering if the cops found any new evidence. With each new day, that fear becomes more tangible, more real.

I consider having another drink, but before I can decide, I hear the doorbell. I frown. It's eight in the evening. Who the hell could it be now?

I walk over and open the door.

"Grace?" I say her name as if she's the last person I expect to see.

In a way, she is. But I notice that she doesn't like the tone of my voice. She's never been able to hide how she felt about something. Bobby never paid much attention to that. I guess Bobby never paid much attention to many things about her, but I did. I thought she annoyed me before, but a strange fear materialized in me lately. What if I was annoyed by the mere fact that she chose him and not me? Truth be told, she was introduced to him first, but still. She was with him, even after meeting me.

"Are you busy?" she asks, and I realize that my mind's been racing, while we're both still standing with the door open.

I step aside to let her in. "Of course, of course," I nod quickly. "Sorry about that. I'm just... a fucking mess right now."

"I can imagine," she replies softly, and I close the door behind her.

She walks into the living room. She looks around, wondering where to sit. Then, she does so on the sofa. The same place where we made love the last time she was here.

Made love. How strange. I usually wouldn't use that word. I'd use anything else, just not made love.

"I spoke with my boss," she suddenly says, her hands in her lap. Her fingers crack barely noticeably. She sometimes did that when she was very nervous. That means she is very nervous now.

"Did you have any problems because of me?" I immediately ask.

"No, no, it's not that," she clarifies, inhaling deeply, as if it requires a lot of physical effort of her to do so.

Her hair is loose, falling down her back. She is wearing barely any make up. She probably didn't go home to change, because she's wearing a white blouse, with pearl buttons and navy blue pants. She's bending slightly forward, and her V-neck opens into a sight I'd love to sink in, but I can't think about that now. She is more beautiful than any other woman I've seen before, but I have to focus. I have to stay level-headed.

"What is it then?" I ask, remembering what she just said.

"He told me that the cops think it's you," she shares something I already know. "They're just waiting to find an incriminating piece of evidence so they can close the case and have someone to blame."

I sigh heavily, raking my fingers through my hair. I fight the urge to pace about the room, and instead, I stay in one place. I focus my attention on her. In this tangled mess of shit, I somehow managed to get myself into, she is the only beacon of hope. She is the only thing keeping me afloat.

I realize that if she wasn't here, I'd feel... lost. It's as simple as that. She calms me down, without even knowing the effect she has on me. And I'm the asshole who's just using her to find out what her boss knows about the case.

"And Mr. Jennings said that he thinks it's probably going to end like that," she finally adds the thing that she's been most concerned about, almost as if she's able to read my mind. "With the cops just focusing on you, and not even taking anyone else into consideration."

"Then we'll have to take someone else into consideration," I nod. "I just don't know who."

I sigh heavily, turning to her. "This is really difficult for me, regardless of what anyone will have you believe." She doesn't say anything to that. I lift my gaze to meet hers. "I wish I had your cat here right now. She is a great stress relief."

This time, she laughs loudly. That noise fills the room around us, making it less solitary, and me, less desperate for some reason. Things still aren't clear between us, but I have the feeling that sometimes, there are flickers of moments that allow me to believe I'm not such an asshole, that I'm not only taking advantage of her, but that I'm actually spending time with her in this way because I like to, and that it has nothing to do with finding out the truth about what happened.

"She is... a very special cat, that's all I'll say," she is still chuckling when she says that.

"Must be nice coming home to her," I point out.

"It is," she confirms, walking around the room, and carefully looking at everything that interests her. As for me, she is the only thing in this room of any interest to me.

She stops in front of a painting of a naked woman, but it's done in chalk, and unless you really peer into the drawing, you can't really tell what it is. She looks at it for a few moments, then she turns back to me.

"I never thought you were an animal lover," she says, sounding surprised.

I shrug. "There are many things you don't know about me." The moment I say it, I know how egotistical it sounds. It will only strengthen her previous belief that I think the whole world revolves around me. So, I quickly add, to even things out. "Just like there are many things I don't know about you."

"Are there?" she asks, amused.

"Of course," I nod.

"I always thought I was an open book," she replies, turning to the drawing again, probably for a more introspective look.

I walk over to her and stand next to her. "That's only about things you want others to know about you," I tell her my view of things. "But you keep the most important things about yourself hidden away."

"Isn't that how everyone works?" she wonders, not taking her eyes off of the drawing.

"Probably," I nod, both of us focused on the same thing. "But you being here isn't a good idea."

I'm not sure why I say this, when her presence is the only thing keeping me from reaching for another glass of whiskey. It's not a good idea because she might get in trouble at work. It's not a good idea because I might not be able to keep my hands off of her. It might not be a good idea for many reasons that I don't even want to list right now, but I know them all. Still, she's here.

She turns to me and smiles. I can't remember the last time someone smiled at me like that. I'm used to people smiling at me all the fucking time. In fact, they do it so much that I thought I forgot how to differentiate between a real smile and a fake one. But this one I recognize immediately.

"No price is too high to pay for finding out the truth," she tells me again.

It's the same thing, only said in different words.

"But this isn't your fight," I remind her, not because I want to antagonize her, but on the contrary. I want to keep her safe from the mess I pulled her into.

"I made it my fight," she corrects me.

"No," I shake my head, sighing, moving away from her. "If your boss finds out, you'll never get another job like that."

"Well," she keeps smiling at me. "Then, you'll have to give me a job at your company."

I'm not sure if she's serious or just joking. She must be joking. Not that I wouldn't give her a job. That goes without saying. But that she would risk it all for me. I can't imagine anyone doing that. Anyone but Bobby, but he's my brother. She is... well, not family. She isn't even someone I would have considered close a month ago. This whole thing blossomed into something unexpected, something I can't quite figure out or even explain to myself.

Sometimes, I think I'm still just using her. People like me aren't meant to love someone. I proved this to myself more than once before. I'm too selfish. I'm too much of an asshole to think about someone else, when I have myself and my own needs to consider first. I always thought I would live my life as an eternal bachelor, never really growing tired of it.

Now, I'm not tired of anything. It's just that Grace managed to find a way through my defenses, through all the walls I've built around myself, and she wants to see past the veil of shit I have surrounding me. She is still here, and that is the most astounding thing for me.

"You know, this could end very badly," I tell her, not only referring to myself.

"I know," she nods. "You could end up in prison, even on death row."

Something clenches at my throat the moment she mentions it. It's true. I just don't want to consider that horrible possibility.

"You could end up getting fired and even being prosecuted for what you're doing," I remind her.

She shrugs. "Compared to what you're facing, mine doesn't seem that bad."

She is smiling again, and it is impossible not to smile back at her.

Seeing her here, I thought I would want to fuck her. I thought that would be the first thing on my mind, but it's not. I just want her to stay here. I just want to listen to her voice even if she's talking about fucking classical music. I wouldn't care. It's the tone of her voice, that melodiousness that I want to absorb into me and let it lull me to sleep.

"Well..." she suddenly says, getting up. "It's pretty late."

"Stay," I rush to tell her. She looks at me, puzzled, silently asking what the reason behind this might be. "I... It's not because I want to fuck you."

Her brows knit even more now, and I realize I'm being confused and awkward, something that never happened to me, at least not around women.

"I mean, I do," I say, but I realize that I'm just digging a deeper grave for myself here. Despite that, she smiles. "That didn't come out right," I grin at her. "What I meant to say was that you could stay, and I could order some dinner. I haven't eaten since lunch, and it's nine now."

She ponders for a few moments, then nods. "I guess I could stay for an hour or so."

"Great," I say, a part of me completely surprised at the direction in which this is going.

You could talk more about the case, that little voice inside of me says. After all, that's why she came here, isn't it?

That's true, but the strange thing is that with her, I want to forget all about the case and not talk about it all the time. I want to listen to her tell me about her day, about her stupid cat that I've grown to like much more than I should. I want to have a normal conversation with her, and not the one revolving around a dead girl found in my weekend house.

She gazes at me as if she can read my thoughts. For a moment, I actually think she does. But then, I remind myself it's just the way she sympathizes. Her eyes are full of understanding and her lips are stuck in a perpetual half-smile, so no matter what you say, it seems she either agrees or understands why you did what you did.

"So, what are you in the mood for?" I grab my phone in an effort to change the topic of conversation.

"I'm not sure," she shrugs. "Any suggestions?"

"Depending on how hungry you are," I tell her my philosophy. "Sushi if you're just a bit hungry, red meat if you're starving. Everything else falls into the middle category of what you're in the mood for."

I chuckle and she joins in. "I like that explanation, although I'm still not sure. Maybe sushi? I've never actually tried it."

"Never!?" I gasp. "Well, then, Missy, you're in for a treat."

She watches me dial a number and order sushi for dinner. I pretend like I don't know that she's not taken her eyes off me even for a second. I also pretend like I don't care.

But that's just it. We're both playing pretend, and I don't know how long we'll be able to play it like that, before someone gets hurt.

Chapter Fifteen

Grace

Surprisingly, there was no sex.

Not that I wanted it. Well, I both wanted it and didn't. That's the curse of being a woman, wanting two things at the same time. But I guess the fact that we didn't make love last night showed me that there is more to this, whatever it is that we have.

Those are my thoughts the following morning when I head to the office. Just as I arrive, I notice that Mr. Jennings is already there.

"Grace, I need you to run over to the courthouse and pick up some documents I left there," he instructs me.

That will take at least an hour to get there, and another hour back. As for in between, that depends on many factors. Suddenly, I get an idea.

"Am I in a rush to return?" I wonder.

He lifts his eyebrow at me. "Why?"

"Well, I was wondering if I could maybe have my lunch break in the meantime, then come back once I'm done," I suggest.

"I don't see why not," he smiles at me.

"Thank you," I smile back. "I have my phone on me, so if you need anything else, just let me know," I add.

"I think that'll be all," he assures me, then once again, his eyes delve into the laptop screen in front of him, and I know it's my cue to leave.

That idea won't let me be. It might not work. She might not be available, especially because she works nights and sleeps during the day. But it's worth a shot. If anyone knows something about those parties, it's her.

As soon as I'm out of the building, I call her. It rings several times. Nothing. She doesn't pick up.

Oh, come on, I think to myself. But I'm not angry with her. I'm actually angry with myself, because I haven't thought of this sooner. I could have contacted her days ago and set up a meeting.

I try her again, but with the same luck.

Shit. I shake my head at the phone. It's nine in the morning. Of course, she's not up. Of course, she's–

At that moment, she calls me back.

"Julia?" I say as soon as I pick up the phone. That's her real name, although she told me she uses it very sparingly. I guess I can understand that.

"Is your house on fire?" she asks, sounding annoyed.

"No, just – "

"Then, why would you call two times in a row, when you know this is way too early for me?" she asks.

"I know, I know," I say as quickly as I can. "I just really need your help with something. Really." I add that last word to assure her how urgent this is.

I hear her sigh on the other end of the line. "Can we do it later? Like much later?"

"No," I say. "It has to be now. Please."

She sighs again, much more loudly, probably with the intention of me hearing it.

"Where are you?" she asks, and I know she still hasn't agreed.

"I'm heading to the courthouse," I reply. "I should be there in about an hour."

She seems to think about it for a moment, then she continues. "There's a little café on the corner of Brogues and Fifth Street. It's called... uhm... shit... what's the name?"

"I don't know, but I'll find it," I assure her.

"It's some shitty mint green place with a red door," she explains. "Fucking hell. What's the name?"

I smile at the description regardless of the swearing. I know it's nothing personal. With Julia, it never is.

"Shitty mint green place with a red door," I repeat, suppressing a chuckle. "I think I'll find it easily enough, no worries."

"OK," she agrees. "An hour?"

"Make it hour and a half, so you don't wait for me if the traffic is bad," I say.

"Fine," she replies curtly, without any appreciation of my suggestion. Again, I know it's nothing personal. "I'll be there. See ya."

Without waiting for me to say anything back, she hangs up. I can't stop smiling. I honestly can't understand why I haven't thought of this earlier. My heart is beating inside my throat, as I try to quickly round up all the questions I want to ask her when I see her.

I head to the courthouse first. The traffic is light. After all, it's the middle of the workday. I pick up the documents in question, and I realize that I'm half an hour early to our rendezvous. Not that I mind. The place is actually very nice, not at all a shitty mint green, but a rather pleasant minty hue. The door, however, looks like the entrance to Hell. Although a bit of contrast is something people will remember. It won't blend in with all the other beige, retro chic cafes that this city is teaming with.

I order a coffee and a bagel, not because I'm all that hungry, but because I want to fill in the waiting time with something. I slowly sip my coffee and eat my bagel, thinking about the questions. I soon realize that I'm fidgeting. I can't seem to sit still, in one place.

I check the clock on the wall. Fifteen minutes more.

I try to do some people watching, in order to calm down my nerves. But nothing seems to work. My attention keeps going back to the door, then to the clock, counting the minutes. Finally, she's here. I raise my hand as soon as I see her walk into the café. She nods, goes to pick up a coffee for herself, and a minute later, she is seated opposite me.

Julia is a woman of about my age, although she seems older. There are dark circles around her eyes, and her usually fully dyed hair is showing dark roots out of the ash blonde. Her nails are bitten to the bone. No extensions this time. She is wearing an oversized short-sleeved t-shirt, without a bra. I can tell. Anyone can tell, but she doesn't seem to mind. Her jeans are of usual cut, slightly above the ankle, revealing some flesh, then her foot slides into a white sneaker. She has no purse or any bag with her.

"Hey," she says, as she sits down, then puts the coffee cup on the table that separates us.

"Thanks for coming," I tell her, not taking my eyes off of her.

"You said it was urgent," she shrugs.

I know she thinks that she still owes me for helping her that one time, although I've forgotten all about that. She's one of those people who will help you five times back for you helping them out once, just so she wouldn't feel like she owes you anything.

"It is," I nod, glancing around. There aren't many people here, and even those who are here seem to be preoccupied with their own conversations.

"What is it?" she asks, not being one for small talk.

I guess she wouldn't be. We aren't friends or anything. But something tells me she generally doesn't like to waste time talking about the weather or the kind of music she likes to listen to. I can respect that.

"I need you to tell me about the parties at Stanton villa," I tell her, lowering my voice, and instinctively leaning over the table, closer to her.

Her face was relaxed when she came in. But now, hearing Jesse's surname, her eyes widen. She doesn't say anything at first.

She looks to her left, then her right. That shocked expression has taken residence in her eyes, and I know it won't go away any time soon.

"It's because of Lucy, isn't it?" she asks her own question instead of replying to mine.

"Mhm," I nod. There is no point in telling her otherwise. She knows where I work and what I do, what my boss does. That is, after all, how we met. "Did you know her?"

I'm only asking because it's been established that Lucy Romero was a professional escort. Not the corner hooker type, though, but a real class act. She would wear Gucci and Prada to her dates, she spoke three languages and she was drop dead gorgeous. Julia belonged to the same circle. At least, she used to. Then, she started to meddle with drugs, and it took its toll, as it always did. Now, there was barely any trace of that sophisticated escort from years back. I hate to even think about what she does now.

"Not that well," she starts, her voice also down to a whisper, so I have to lean in even closer. "I've seen her around, at… places." She hesitates.

"Places like… that villa?" I try to follow her lead. She doesn't want to mention names and places, and I can understand why.

"Mhm," she confirms.

"Were you ever there yourself?" I ask.

"Mhm," she nods again. "It was crazy."

"Crazy how?" I frown.

She looks around again. "You know," she whispers. "Celebrities, or at least people who like to think themselves so. And girls. Always lots of pretty, young girls."

"Alcohol?" I wonder, although I know the answer to that.

"A shitload," she tells me. "That and… drugs." The last word is barely audible. But I can read her lips well.

"Everything?" I ask again. She just nods silently. "Who organized them?"

She grimaces with her lips. "I don't know. The billionaire? His brother?"

"Didn't you know?" I ask, sounding a bit incredulous.

"I didn't care," she shrugs. "And neither did anyone else who was there, as long as they had booze and drugs."

"Aha," I nod, although this is something I knew myself. "I was hoping you'd tell me something more specific."

She shakes her head. "I haven't been there this year at all." She seems to wonder whether to explain why, then she opts for it. "I haven't been invited."

"Why?" I ask.

She gestures at her body. "I wasn't up to the standard anymore, I guess. Not in this condition."

I know what she means, but I bite my tongue before I say anything.

"Do you know any girls who were there? Someone I can talk to?" I wonder, but I know it's a farfetched idea.

"No one will talk to you, Grace," she gives me her honest opinion. "Not with Lucy dead and the cops still trying to figure out who did it. I mean, it's probably the billionaire. Who else could it be? And if it's him, I know I'd also want to lay low and not run my tongue where it doesn't belong."

She grabs her coffee cup and brings it to her lips, taking a sip. I notice a small crack in the corner of her lips. Could be just a case of badly chapped lips or maybe someone slapped her. It wouldn't be the first time.

"What about you, Julia?" I ask. "How are you doing?"

"I'm fine," she replies, realizing we're done talking about Lucy and now we're up her alley. She doesn't like that. She downs her entire coffee, which must be still hot, but doesn't even blink. "Is that all?"

"Yeah, but– " I try, but she doesn't let me finish.

"Don't involve me in this, Grace," she asks, in a tone unlike her usual. She is pleading. She would never plead, not even if her life depended on it. "Keep me out of it."

I don't say anything. Before she goes, I slide a hundred across the table to her, hidden under the palm of my hand. She hesitates, before taking it. Her lips part. There is something on her mind, but it remains buried in there.

She lifts her hand to me, then disappears through those red doors, for some people, the entrance to Hell, for others, the exit.

Chapter Sixteen

Jesse

That night, Grace isn't at my place. I'm at hers.

Titi is purring in my lap, something I never thought I would enjoy again. But I guess this is a period of change. Some of it good, some less so. I have an indescribable urge to light up a cigarette, but I fight it. Maybe I could even quit for real this time.

"The parties?" I ask, after she told me everything she found out from that source of hers, although it wasn't much. At least, it's nothing new, nothing that would be of any help. "Everyone knows about the parties."

"Even the cops?" she wonders.

"Well, of course," I nod. "How do you think this functions?"

She frowns. Maybe not a good choice of words on my part.

"How would I know?" she replies, a little venomously. "I've never been to any of your infamous parties, nor am I a billionaire."

"That's not what I meant," I tell her calmly, trying to extinguish this fire. "Just... I thought everyone knows. I mean, you have to have some back up. People do drugs there. Serious drugs. They bring escorts there. You know, girls who are paid to sleep with whomever is in the mood?"

She doesn't seem very satisfied with my explanation.

"Did you do it?" she suddenly asks, her voice low and lacking in confidence, as if she's wondering whether she should even be asking this.

"Did I do what?" I ask her in return.

"Drugs," she explains.

I exhale awkwardly. How do you reply to such a question?

I don't want her to think badly of me, but the truth is that of course, I tried some of it. Most of it, actually. However, I was lucky enough to know not to continue with that, because I know that shit isn't good for me. Others weren't so lucky.

Should I lie? Best not to.

But dammit, why do I care about her opinion so much? I shouldn't care at all. She's just here to help clear my name, to tell me everything I need to know, everything that the DA will know and where the investigation is heading. I shouldn't care about her opinion of me.

Yes, I fucking did drugs. That is what I should reply, but I don't.

"I did," I say simply instead. I shrug, as if I were helpless in this act, but that's not true and we both know it. "I'm not proud of it, but I wouldn't go so far as to call it a mistake. Life is out there for you to try, and you decide what is good for you and what isn't. The truth is that drugs aren't for everyone. I mean, it's not for anyone, if you think about it, but I know people who function very well, and they've been smoking pot for years. They handle their stress like that. Now, I'm not saying we should all get high when shit hits the fan, but..."

"But it's a good option?" she chuckles.

At least I made her smile. That's a small victory as well.

"I have no idea what are good options anymore," I admit. "I just know that it's been two weeks, and I'm no closer to finding out what's gonna happen or who the real perpetrator is."

"Don't worry," she smiles at me. "We'll solve this... together."

If I heard this from anyone else, I'd think them horribly pathetic. But coming from her, it makes sense. It sounds soothing, and I'm grateful for that.

"I just have the feeling that the cops will be knocking on my door any day now, to arrest me. I even dreamt that," I confess, feeling the burden of that overwhelming dream once again.

"I can't convince you that it won't happen, because we both know it's a possibility," she says softly. "But I can tell you to stay confident and optimistic."

"I appreciate that," I sigh. "As for those parties, I wish I could somehow prove that I haven't been there in ages. I know that Bobby and that buddy of his kept asking to have parties there."

"Is it possible that someone somehow gained access to it without you knowing?" she asks. "Without either of them knowing?"

"Of course," I nod, shrugging. "I mean, everyone knows I'm in the city all the time. I have a business to take care of. Buying that villa was something I didn't even need. I can see that now. But I didn't know that back then, when all that mattered was to show off my wealth."

"It's OK," she replies. "You haven't done anything wrong by buying a house you barely use. You aren't the first and I'm sure you won't be the last one."

"But that's just it," I continue. "It served no purpose and now, it only got me in trouble."

"It was what you wanted," she reassures me. "There is no point in feeling bad about something you wanted. It's done. It's in the past. You have to look towards the future now."

"Yeah," I nod. "Only my future doesn't look that bright right now."

"Everyone has problems," she just doesn't want to let me drown in self-pity. A part of me appreciates it. Another part just wants her to allow me to do this, but I know it's not a good idea. My circle of self-pity usually ends in rage. I don't want to be angry around her.

I expect her to continue, but she doesn't say anything else. Instead, she seems like she's thinking about something. Then, a moment later, she continues.

"Have you been there since it happened?" I hear her ask.

"At the villa?"

"Mhm," she nods.

"No," I admit. "I don't think I want to."

"But why?"

I frown. "What do you mean why?"

"The police were there, right?" she asks again. I just nod this time. "Maybe they overlooked something."

I frown again. "They're the police. It's their job not to overlook anything."

"All I'm saying is that they were looking for evidence to incriminate you, not for evidence of someone else in the house, right?" she asks, and I have to agree with her.

Judging from her boss' words and generally by how these things go, this is more than possible. The idea of justice is such a fickle thing nowadays. We live in a world where money can buy anything, even guilt or innocence.

"So, what are you saying?" I ask.

"I'm saying we should go to your weekend house and see for ourselves if there's something they might have overlooked," she finally says what's on her mind.

The thought of going there, knowing what happened, doesn't sit right. She sees the expression on my face, and she recognizes it instantly.

"You don't want to go?"

"Not really," I admit. "Not knowing what happened there."

"But they took the body," she points out.

"Perhaps," I shake my head. "But I doubt they cleaned the blood from the carpets or wherever it was."

Still, I know that she's right. It would be a good thing to go there and comb through the house. Maybe we could manage to find something that they didn't notice. It wouldn't be the first time the police didn't do their job properly.

However, I still don't like it, although I know we should do it.

"I know how you feel," she suddenly speaks up. "I also wouldn't want to go. But at the same time, I would be curious. You say you haven't been there all year?"

"Mhm," I nod. "Maybe even longer. I honestly don't remember. Time flies sometimes."

"Or..." she seems to ponder another idea. "I could go there without you and– "

"Absolutely not," I refuse. "We go together, or no one goes."

"I was kinda hoping you'd say that," she grins mischievously, trying to lighten up the mood. Somehow, she manages to do it.

I don't know how, but half an hour later, we're already in the car, on the way there. It's a silent drive. I guess we're both considering all the possibilities that might await us there. I'm wondering what I'll find when I open the door.

Will it be like in the movies, with blood spatters everywhere? Or will be disinfected and cleaned? I doubt the latter, but hopefully, it's not as bad as the former. Honestly, I have no idea what to expect and that is the scariest thing.

"What are you thinking about?" she interrupts the silence first.

I just glance at her from the side, gripping at the steering wheel, then I focus my gaze back on the road, which is dark and winding. There is a forest nearby, so I have to be very careful. It's not uncommon for a deer to jump out in front of a car. And that's the last thing I need right now, for something to happen to us both, especially to Grace.

"The villa," I admit curtly. I figure she will ask me something else about it, but her question surprises me. Once again, she is trying to lighten up the mood with questions that steer the conversation towards a more normal topic.

"Will you sell it when all of this is over?" she wonders.

I grin at the idea. "I doubt anyone would want to buy it, seeing someone died there... violently."

"Well, if you think about it like that, someone died in every single house in the world," she says knowledgeably.

I have to chuckle at her remark. "Point taken."

"Also, some people are really into it," she continues, and it is again to distract us both from what we're about to do. Even though I don't say it, I'm grateful for her presence. "They'd happily take it off your hands."

"After all this is done, I don't want anything to do with it," I tell her something she already knows. "I'll probably put it up for sale. Hell, I might even give it to someone who wants it."

She doesn't say anything to that. She just smiles one of those rare, somehow sad smiles. We continue the drive for the next fifteen minutes in silence again, after which we arrive. I stop the car and get out first. She doesn't wait for me to open the door for her. I'm not sure if she didn't expect me to or didn't want me to. I guess that doesn't matter at a time like this.

We both stand in front of the house, which under any other circumstances would have been Heaven on Earth. Of course, it is, because I made it with that very same intent in mind. Trying to keep the local character, I restored a house that was already there, only adding to it a little. On the other side, where Grace can't see yet, there is a decked area, which was meant to overlook the valley. I spent many peaceful mornings there, just sipping my coffee and enjoying the sound of nature, being away from the hustle and bustle of the city.

I don't know why, but I expected it all to be different. I expected even nature to be appalled by what happened, resulting in some horrible, visible change. Instead, I've come here to find everything the same. Nature keeps on flowing, as if nothing's happened, and suddenly, that fear grips me harder than the fear of being locked up for the rest of my life, or even worse. The saddest part is that Lucy Romero's death changed nothing here. Apart from her family and close friends, who will mourn her? Who will mourn any of us?

Just as those thoughts swarm inside my mind, pricking me painfully, I feel Grace's reassuring touch on my shoulder.

"Are you OK?" she whispers softly.

I inhale deeply, nodding. "Yeah."

I don't know if that's true. I guess it doesn't matter, because we have to do this. There is no other way. We have to find out who killed that girl, not for my sake, but for her own as well.

Chapter Seventeen

Grace

He unlocks the door and opens it for me. I dare not go inside first.

He obviously senses my hesitation and enters, then I follow him, closing the door behind us. We walk through a small hallway, which leads right into the spacious living area, which is done in a very modernist style. It is centered around a fireplace, and I can imagine what he had in mind with it: peaceful evenings without any intrusions. Then, how come this became a party place?

All the furniture and other details are pastel, done in a contemporary style, with an occasional pop of a bright, almost neon color, which adds vivacity to the whole place. I wonder if he did it himself or if he hired an interior decorator. Before I can make up my mind on this one, I see it.

It's in the corner, so we couldn't notice it immediately upon entering. But now, standing in the middle of the room, we both see it.

There is a big stain on the carpet, and faint outlines of the body done in chalk. They didn't even bother to clean it all up properly.

We're both looking in that direction, unable to say anything. I want to ask him again if he's OK, but I get the idea I've asked him this too many times already. Instead, I just stand by his side. Instinctively, I move to take him by the hand. I don't know how he'll react. Maybe he'll push it away. Maybe he doesn't want me to show affection and tenderness, but I have to try.

I take him by the hand. A moment passes by, then another one. Our fingers intertwine. He squeezes my hand and I squeeze his back. We stand like that for a few more moments, then he pulls away. He walks over to where the stains are and looks at them but doesn't bend down. I go near him as well.

"This is what she looked like?" he asked.

"Probably," I nod, staring at the outline.

"It's a good thing I didn't come sooner," I hear him say.

I can tell this shook him. I've never been here before, but it has the same effect on me as well. Somehow eerie, a feeling that something bad happened here, something this house will never be able to erase from its past.

"Come," I say, realizing that we could be standing like this for the next couple of hours, focused on that stain and thinking about what happened, what could have happened and will never happen. "We'd best focus on searching the place."

"You're right," he says, pulling away, as if from a reverie. "Should we... separate, like in detective movies?" he asks, managing to provoke a chuckle out of me.

"That means one of us will die, you know," I remind him of horror movies.

"Good point," he nods. "No separation then."

"No," I agree. "Wherever we go, we go together."

"What about the bathroom?" he asks, and I realize he's also doing his best to lighten up the situation.

"We go there alone," I explain, unable to resist chuckling to this as well.

"Well," he looks around, "I suppose we start here."

He starts pacing about the living room aimlessly. "So, what are we looking for?" he asks.

I do the same thing as he. I realize I've never done this before. I thought it would be easy. In movies and TV shows, they always make it look so easy. The evidence you're looking for is exactly in plain sight of you, but no one else. You find it and the case simply starts to unravel on its own.

That is, however, not the case here. We pace about the room, searching for something, but not really sure exactly what. When you have no idea what you're looking for, finding it becomes all the more difficult.

We move from this room to the kitchen. It is a sand-colored kitchen, with lots of space. The windows are huge, and although now it's dark and the curtains are drawn, I can imagine that lots of sunlight comes in, making this one of the brightest rooms in the entire house.

I look around, half-expecting to find bottles and glasses, but everything seems put away. Nothing is amiss. It's as if someone came here and cleaned up the entire place. I wonder if the cops found any fingerprints. That's how clean the place looks. Not only cleaned, but actually disinfected.

"This feels pointless," I hear him say with a heavy sigh. "We're just walking around doing nothing."

"I know that's how it feels," I try to reassure him. "But we're looking for... something."

"I wish I knew what that something looked like," he admitted, bending down behind the kitchen counter, opening cupboards and peering inside. However, he'd close every single one of them with the same look on his face.

"Me, too," I nod, focused on the area around me.

"I'm dying for a cigarette now," he suddenly says, stopping and patting his pockets.

"Didn't you stop?" I glance over at him, as he picks out a cigarette from the pack and puts it in the corner of his lips. "Back when..." I don't finish my sentence, although we both know what I'm referring to. I meant, back when I was still with Bobby.

Bobby used to tease him about this special brand of cigarettes that Jesse used to smoke. No others were good enough, but these. I wrack my brain trying to remember the name.

Treasurer Luxury Black. Yes, those are the ones. Some people do not make that much money in a month, and he spent that much on one pack of cigarettes. That's what Bobby always used to say. Jesse didn't mind, of course. His come back was that it was his money, and he could spend it any damn way he pleased. He always used to have such a comeback, which didn't make him a very likeable guy.

However, it seems that the guy I'm starting to get to know is the person he used to be before acquiring all that money, that made him paranoid, that made him fearful of people who would stab him in the back, so in order to have control over everything, he had to become someone else, someone different, someone ruthless.

I never understood that. Never until now.

He lights up the cigarette in his mouth, inhaling with great satisfaction. His eyes are closed. He is fully in the moment.

"I did quit," he tells me. "But that was before this happened." He gestures at the house around him. "I needed something to calm down my nerves, so I took it up again."

"Well, that's not good," I frown.

"Tell me about it," he says, inhaling again.

He walks over to the nearest window and opens it wide. He turns his back to me and leans outward. Some of the chilly night air seeps in, mixing with the smoke. I don't mind it, but obviously he does.

At that moment, I look down at my feet. Underneath the kitchen island, pushed all the way down, is a half-smoked cigarette. I glance at him, then I quickly bend down and pick it up. It is the same as his. There is no doubt about it.

He is still with his back to me. I should show him. I should ask him about it. But I'm afraid what the answer might be. I'm afraid that he won't have an explanation or that it will be farfetched and unbelievable.

That is why I shove the cigarette into my pocket, having no idea what I want to do with it.

When he turns around to face me, I feel like my heart is beating inside my throat. He finishes his cigarette, then extinguishes it in the sink. He continues to look for... something, and we move from room to room. I follow him as if in a daze, thinking about the cigarette in my pocket and what it could mean.

I know he's telling the truth about not being here. I just know it. I feel it in my bones. I've never been so sure about anything else. But I'm still afraid to face him and ask him about it.

It takes us about three hours to go over every room, silently, not that slowly, though. At one point, I've noticed that he's had enough. It all seems pointless, and I guess I understand him.

"There," he says when we're done. "We didn't find anything."

Now. Tell him now. That little voice inside of me is urging me to show him what I found. Just as I'm on the verge of doing so, something pulls me back and the cigarette remains safely tucked into my pocket.

"It was worth a shot," I shrug.

"I guess," he replies, but he doesn't sound convinced at all.

We stand in the doorway for a moment, then he locks the door behind us. He sounds and looks defeated as we head back to the car. The drive back is even more silent. Neither of us makes any small talk. The radio is the only thing filling the void between us, but we're not listening to the music. We're both lost in our own thoughts.

He drops me off at my place. When he stops the car, he turns to me.

"Thanks," he says, his voice serious and somehow solemn. "For coming with me."

"Sure thing," I nod.

I consider telling him about the cigarette here as well, but I know that I'll have more to explain if I do so. I'll have to tell him why I kept it a secret on the ride back, why I didn't show it to him in the first place. So, again, just like before, I opt against it. I don't want him to think that I don't trust him, but at the same time, there is some suspicion in me. I'm just not certain what it's about.

Because this cigarette doesn't have to be his. After all, everyone knows he smokes this particular brand. It could be yet another trick to try and frame him for something he didn't do. I have to find out.

I lean over and kiss him on the cheek. That seems the safest thing right now. I don't invite him to come upstairs, nor does he offer to. It's almost morning. Fortunately, tomorrow is Saturday, and I can stay in bed all morning, cuddling with Titi. If, of course, she lets me.

I wave at him and get out of the car. I rush into my apartment building and a minute later, I'm locking the door from the inside. My heart is beating wildly. I take out the cigarette from my pocket, examining it. I honestly don't know what I expect to see with the naked eye, but just looking at it gives me a strange sense of power over the situation. Almost as if I'm holding a vital clue in my hands, but I just don't know it yet.

I don't even take a shower. I'm too tired to do so. I head to my bedroom and slump onto the bed. As soon as I close my eyes, I fall asleep. As always, Titi nestles cozily at the foot of the bed, and we sleep together like that until noon.

Chapter Eighteen

Jesse

I wake up the following day around noon, feeling completely broken, as if I haven't slept a wink.

I was hoping that visiting the villa would provide me with some insight if not answers, but it turns out that the trip was done in vain. We didn't discover anything.

Without any appetite, I make myself a coffee, but even that tastes like shit. I know it has nothing to do with the coffee itself, but rather my state of mind. Staying home will only make things worse. I won't be able to escape my own mind. Maybe if I go to work and focus on something that needs to be done, that will keep me occupied enough before I go crazy.

Hoping that working will save my mind from going mad, I head to the office. I reach it fairly quickly. The traffic on Saturdays is pretty smooth, despite that one accident that happened. Luckily, the radio was on, so I knew to go the roundabout way, which still saved me time.

When I arrive at work, I nod at the security guard. He waves back at me.

"No rest for the rich, Mr. Stanton?" he asks jokingly, as always.

"You know it, Willie," I smile back.

"That's why I'm here, boss," he winks at me with that lazy eye of his. "We rich folks know the importance of hard work."

"Just for that, Willie, you get to go home today to tell your wife you're getting a raise," I smile, pointing my index finger at him, as I head for the elevators.

"Oh, the Missus will be mighty pleased to hear that," he replies. "Thank you, Mr. Stanton!"

"Don't mention it," I tell him, but the doors to the elevator are already closed.

This is actually the second time I'll be doing this for old Willie. He and his wife remind me of the grandparents that I never had, the grandparents I always dreamed of. They unfortunately never had any kids of their own, his wife had ovarian cancer in her early twenties, and almost died. She survived but was told she would never have kids. Willie even said she tried leaving him because she knew he would never leave her first. But sometimes, love conquers all. Not always though. Just sometimes.

I have to remember to up his pay immediately. Yes. That will be one of the things today to keep me busy and focused on anything other than the fact that my freedom might be hanging by a thread. A very thin thread that might be cut at any moment.

I ride the elevator to the last floor, where I enter my office. I like it when the building is empty, save for a few people. Usually, it is packed, which is of course to be expected. You can't run a multimillion dollar company with just a handful of people. You need hundreds of them for hundreds of jobs.

I sit down at my laptop and go over the financial statements, when I notice more of what I've been noticing in the past couple of weeks. There is money missing. And not a small amount. There are payments to companies I've never heard of and to people as well. Usually, I have other people to handle this, but when it's a larger amount, I always need to be kept in the loop on who gets how much. That's always been my rule. If you allow other people full reign over your finances, you're bound to get cheated on. That's why I always check, especially amounts like these.

I scroll through rows and rows of payments, but none of this seems to make any sense. The only thing I can figure out is that money is somehow leaking out of the company. And the worst part is that I don't know how.

I get up, raking my fingers through my hair. I light up a cigarette, vowing that this will be my last one. This is, of course, a lie. I know it won't be, but thinking so makes it easier for me. It soothes me into thinking I'm not addicted to them, but rather just indulging a momentary desire. Nothing else.

I pace about my office, wondering how the fuck I got myself in this mess. How come I didn't see it coming?

But... see what? I still have no idea what's going on. There's no way I could have predicted it. Still, I have to deal with it, any way I know how.

There is only one person I want to talk to right now. She probably won't have any idea how to help, but just talking to her soothes me. It'll help put my mind at ease and maybe then, something will come to me. Something good.

I grab my phone, a new one, and call Grace. I consider the fact that maybe she's sleeping. After all, we came back pretty late, or pretty early, depending on how one looks at it. She is out of this mess. She should be able to get a good night's rest, unlike me.

However, she picks up on the second ring.

"Yes?" she answers, and the moment I hear her voice, something inside of me clenches. I have no idea what this is. I just know that it's not something ordinary, something that happens with every other woman.

"Did I wake you?" I ask.

"No," she replies. "I was just lounging."

"Wanna have breakfast?" I ask, then I realize the time for breakfast is long past. "I mean, lunch. Or brunch. Or just... do you wanna go grab something to eat?"

She hesitates. I wonder if she's smiling at my awkwardness.

Maybe she's wondering what happened to me. This isn't me. This isn't the persona I've created for everyone to see, for everyone to fear and respect. This awkward guy is the child in me that I had to leave behind when I became a billionaire. You can't be ruthless and still nurture that innocence inside of you. Those two are mutually exclusive. So, I had to make a choice. One of them had to go. Unfortunately, it was the child in me, the one who was still in awe of everything, not in a materialistic sort of way, but who was amazed by life itself and all it had to offer.

Money substituted that awe for me and now I find that nothing puts me in that moment of awe. Nothing but Grace. Little by little, I've come to realize that she is the one bringing out the best in me. With her belief and her tender affection, she is pulling that child out of hiding, gently leading him by the hand.

"I'd love that," she finally says. "Pick me up?"

"Sure," I nod. "Be there in half an hour."

"I'll be ready," she replies. "See ya then."

"Bye," I hang up.

Half an hour later, I'm right on time.

"Where do you want to go?" I ask, as she's fastening her seatbelt.

"Somewhere... cozy," she says, and I can't help but chuckle.

"What do you mean cozy?" I start the car and we head in the general direction of the city center.

"I mean somewhere where they don't know you by name and you won't get special treatment," she explains unapologetically.

"Oooh, yeah, that makes sense," I nod.

"I was actually thinking of picking something up and going to the park to eat it," she suggests.

"I don't remember the last time I did something like that," I admit.

"I figured," she smiles. "With everything going on, I thought you might like something like that."

"That actually sounds like a great idea," I nod. "But... didn't we say we're not supposed to be seen together? I really don't want to get you into any trouble."

"Meh," she shrugs. "I won't hide away like a criminal. Besides, we can go to the park on the other side of the city, you know, the one with the lake?"

"You mean the one where they don't advise you to go at night because of all the drug dealers?" I laugh.

"Yeah, that's exactly the one," she confirms, and we both laugh loudly, almost as if this is nothing but a simple date, and there is no hidden agenda behind this.

Maybe there isn't. I'm not sure anymore.

We pick up some sandwiches and a coffee, and about half an hour later, we're strolling through the park. The sun is shining down on the lush trees. The vibrant flowers are everywhere. The city guys really did a great job at keeping this place nice... at least, during the day. Somehow, at night, it seems to be a completely different place. I've only visited it once at night, and I never want to repeat that experience again. I don't mention any of this to Grace, as we keep heading towards the lake.

There is a small group of guys and girls playing frisbee. They seem like they don't have a care in the world. I guess in your early twenties, it feels like you've got the world by the balls. Then, slowly, you realize it's actually the other way around. But there's little you can do to change anything about it.

When we reach the lake, we sit on the nearest bench, and gaze at the water. It looks like a mirror, with the sun reflecting on its calm surface.

"This is such a nice place," she says softly. "I hate what they've turned it into. I mean, it's famous for drug dealers. Can you imagine?"

"Yeah," I nod in agreement.

She opens the sandwiches, and we start eating in silence. In the distance, there is the sound of kids playing. Maybe there is still hope for this place. Maybe there is hope for us all.

She takes a sip of her coffee, and that is when I tell her.

"Someone is stealing money from my company," I say, without looking at her, but rather still gazing at the distance.

She turns to me. I can feel her gaze burning my cheek. "Do you know who it is?"

"If I did, the motherfucker would already be in prison," I add. "If he's lucky."

"But... you do know what this means, right?" she suddenly asks.

"No, what?" I wonder.

"These two things could be connected," she points out. "Lucy's death and someone stealing from your company. Is it a big sum?"

"I don't know the exact number, but largeish sums have been sent to non-existent companies and names I can't recognize, I'm guessing the overall sum is probably huge."

"Hmmm," she thinks about it for a few moments. "I know this guy who might be able to help, if of course, you're willing to let him look into your financial documents."

"Do you trust him?" I ask.

"Yes," she says, without any hesitation in her voice. "I wouldn't tell you about him unless I was sure of his ability to keep his mouth shut about anything."

"Good," I nod.

"He's a hacker," she explains. "Odds are if there's anyone who can find out who the real recipient of that money is, it's him."

I shrug. "It's worth a shot." I pause for a moment, then I continue. "I have a guy of my own as well, but in this situation, I don't trust anyone. I can't. I think I've lost trust in everyone but you and Bobby. I feel like the entire world is against me, and I don't know where to turn for help."

She smiles, taking me by the hand. "You can turn to me... always."

I smile back at her, feeling that unfamiliar warmth inside my heart, that long forgotten feeling of knowing exactly where I am and who I need to be with. But I can't offer her anything. Not yet. Not with this stain on my name. I have to clear it first and only then can I tell her about my emotions for her. Not before.

"It really means so much to me to have you by my side," I admit. That is already me saying too much. I squeeze her hand back.

"I'll call that guy as soon as I get home," she tells me. "He works fast."

"Can he come tonight?" I ask.

"I have to see with him," she replies. "But as soon as I have something specific, I'll let you know."

"Thanks," I say, gazing back at the lake again. "Do you mind if we stay here a little longer?" I ask, feeling unable to return to that hustle and bustle yet.

Here, I feel like it's a different world. It's peaceful. It's away from everyone and everything.

"We can stay here as long as you'd like," she whispers back, kissing me on the cheek, then leaning her head onto my shoulder.

Birds are chirping in the distance. The sun's reflection is flickering on the surface of the water. For one blissful moment, I am in Heaven, with Grace by my side.

Chapter Nineteen

Grace

"Whoever did this sure hid his tracks well," Jonathan tells us, the reflection of the laptop screen reverberating against his thick-rimmed eyeglasses.

I have the feeling that every time I saw him, his glasses seemed thicker and thicker, as if his eyesight was getting terribly worse from all the time he had to spend stuck in front of a computer screen. But that was his job. Well, sort of.

"Can you find him?" Jesse asks, standing to Jonathan's left side, while I'm standing to his right.

"Yes, but it won't take five minutes, you know," Jonathan turns to us.

I look at the clock on the wall. It's ten in the evening. This will probably be an all nighter.

"Should we order something to eat?" I suggest.

"Pizza is fine," Jonathan tells us again, not taking his eyes off of the screen, his fingers working overtime, clicking in a rhythm that is becoming more and more frantic.

"I'm not hungry," I hear Jesse say.

Jonathan turns to him. "Not now, but you will be in five hours, trust me. This shit takes time and energy. Just order something for yourself, you'll thank me later."

Jesse just nods, and leaves his office, but the door stays open. I follow him into the hallway. It's empty, devoid of any people.

"The suspense is killing me," he admits, raking his fingers through his hair.

He takes out a package of cigarettes and lights one up. I watch the embers burn, as he inhales.

"Is it that good?" I ask, trying out a joke.

He looks at me awkwardly. He doesn't get what I'm referring to immediately. But it dawns on him a moment later.

"Oh," he says, looking at the cigarette nestled between his fingers. "No, not really. It just distracts me from all this shit I'm going through."

I remember the cigarette I found at the villa. I left it at home, still wondering what to do with it. A part of me wants to mention it to him, but it's been too long now. How would I explain holding onto it and not mentioning it? I can't. I have to look into that one on my own and see what I find. In the meantime, we have to focus on Jonathan and what he will discover tonight.

We order some pizza, as per Jonathan's request, then we go back into Jesse's office. Jonathan is still sitting in front of the laptop, scrolling through lines of code that makes sense only to him. There is no point in asking him anything yet. I know that. When he stumbles onto something worth reporting, he'll do so on his own.

Jesse hovers above him, watching Jonathan's fingers dance on the keyboard, working tirelessly to solve this mystery.

"There is a surge in financial transfers that started about three months ago," Jonathan says suddenly, not taking his eyes off the screen. "It is all going to different accounts, but here..." he stops to point at something on the screen, something that seems to make little sense to a layman, but all the sense to him. "This is where you can see it's all going to a single unknown account. You know, like little rivulets coming from all sides, all flowing into one sea."

"So, this is all for the purpose of trying to confuse me and the financial department?" Jesse asks.

"Yup," Jonathan nods, pushing his glasses a bit up his nose with the tip of his middle finger. His eyes narrow as he stares at the screen. "The amount is massive."

"How massive?" Jesse asks again, bending down, as if he understands what he's seeing on the screen. But Jonathan's words are enough to convince him that it's a very serious matter.

"Three million were stolen in just the last three months," Jonathan points out.

"A fuckin mil per month?" Jesse growls. I can see him grinding his teeth. "Who the fuck is it?"

"I can't see yet," Jonathan admits, continuing to type furiously. "But if you give me some time, I might be able to give you a name."

I listen to their conversation, with my heart pounding like crazy. I turn to Jesse.

"This can't be a coincidence," I tell him. "This money missing, and Lucy being murdered. There has to be a connection. We're just not seeing it."

"Usually, your security team would be able to catch this," Jonathan tells us, a bit absent-mindedly. But we both know why that is.

"Unless whoever is doing this is himself in the security team," I point out.

Jonathan stops typing. He looks at me. "Quite possible."

We both turn to Jesse.

"You can't know all the people who work for you," I start first. "But maybe you know who's on your security team?"

Jesse shrugs. "I don't hire them myself. I have a screening process done by other people to decide whether someone is trustworthy to work in such a position."

I don't want to say anything, but that sort of defeats the purpose. Only you can know whether someone is trustworthy. You can't have others decide that for you.

Then, suddenly, something comes to him. "Bobby's best friend, Shawn– "

"Wallace," Jonathan finishes Jesse's sentence.

There is silence for a few moments. We all allow this knowledge to sink in.

"He's appeared three times already," Jonathan explains. "He was using different computers, even in different sections of the company. But you have to sign in, maybe not at the beginning of the transaction, but in order for it to be fulfilled, someone has to authorize it. Since not everyone has that authorization, he had to eventually reveal his identity. Although, he's done a helluva job running me through hoops to get his name."

"He's that good?" Jesse asks.

"Three mil good," Jesse reminds him. "And maybe if we go back even further, we might find more money leakages."

"Don't go back any further," Jesse shakes his head. "This is enough. Do you have enough to bring him down?"

"I don't know," Jonathan admits, once again adjusting his glasses. "I told you, he did a bangin' job of this. If anyone takes a closer look, it looks like just company orders being fulfilled. No big deal."

"But the amounts are too big," Jesse says.

"You know that," Jonathan reminds him. "But the rest of the security team might not. They check only up to a certain point, and before you come to the end of this line, it all looks legit."

"How come I figured out something was wrong?" Jesse keeps wondering.

Jonathan shrugs. "You know what you're looking for. You know your numbers. And it seems your security team sucks."

"No shit, Sherlock," Jesse says, and both Jonathan and I chuckle.

Jesse rakes his fingers through his hair, then turns to Jonathan. "You sure that's the guy? Like, absolutely sure?"

Jonathan nods. "I'd bet my infamous reputation on it."

"Fucking Hell," Jesse curses through his teeth.

I think about it for a moment, then slowly, the pieces of this puzzle start to come together. "You said that your brother and Shawn were the ones organizing parties at your villa, right?" I ask him.

"Mhm," he confirms.

"Is it possible that he somehow gained access to the house without your brother's knowledge?" I ask again.

"Of course," he shrugs. "Bobby is... well, he's not the brightest bulb out there, if you know what I mean. He's a nice guy and nice guys trust everyone. He'd give a stranger the shirt off his back if only he asked for it."

"I know," I smile, remembering Bobby's good traits. "There's not a single doubt in my mind that Bobby isn't involved. It's Shawn."

I remember this guy from before. I saw him once or twice, but I didn't like him from the first moment I laid my eyes on him. It always seemed to me that he was jealous of Bobby, but I wasn't sure why exactly. I even thought he might be hitting on me, but I couldn't tell for sure. That's why I decided that I didn't want that guy around, so every time Bobby wanted us all to hang out together, I would feign some excuse and not go. Bobby, being the good guy that he is, never questioned it, and I never explained it. But that guy never sat right with me. Now, I can see why.

"I can't believe this," Jesse shakes his head. "He's been my brother's friend for years. I never even dreamed he could do something like this."

"Who knows what this guy is capable of," I add. "We should be careful when talking to him. Maybe we should get the police in on this first."

Jonathan immediately stood up. "If you're getting the cops here, I'm bailing. I don't want to have anything to do with this. I'm on probation as it is."

"Of course," I nod at him. "We would never tell of your involvement in this."

"No one is calling the cops," Jesse interrupts us. "This needs to be handled differently. I don't want the cops meddling in my business. They've had their chance to help. They did shit. Now, it's my turn."

"What do you plan to do?" I ask, watching him grab his jacket, and head to the door.

Jonathan and I run after him. We all head to the elevators together.

"I'm going to have a chat with that motherfucker," Jesse growls through clenched teeth. "And demand an explanation."

"Just... calm down," I try to reach him, but I can see that it's too late. He's enraged. I guess I would be as well, so I understand.

The elevator arrives and all three of us go inside, heading down. Jonathan doesn't say anything. He realizes his job here is done. Usually, he asks for some payment when he does this sort of a job, but he owes me a favor, so of course, this one is on the house.

As soon as the elevator opens, Jonathan runs out first, rushing through the front door. The security guy watches him suspiciously, but the moment he sees that Jesse is coming right behind him, he eases up on him.

"Done for tonight, Mr. Stanton?" he asks.

"Only beginning, Willie," Jesse tells the security guard.

Before the guy can say anything else, Jesse heads out the door. I wave at the guy nervously, then run after Jesse.

"Where are you going?" I demand, breathless, as we both reach his car. He grabs the handle to the door but doesn't open it.

"I'm going to Shawn's place," he tells me. "Go back inside. Willie will call you a taxi and go home."

I frown. "I will do no such thing."

"Grace," he snarls, but there is no anger in it, at least not directed at me. "This is no child's play. This guy is dangerous. If he had something to do with that girl's death, I... I can't have you there with me. I wouldn't forgive myself if something happened to you."

"I know you're worried, but I can take care of myself," I remind him. "Besides, we've been in this together all this time, from the beginning. Do you really expect me to let you go on your own without witnessing the unraveling moment myself?"

He sighs heavily, looking at me.

"You know I'll just follow you if you leave me here, right?" I add, for clarification purposes. "It's best to just have me by your side. Who knows, I might actually help you."

"Why are you so stubborn?" he asks, opening the door. "Get in the car."

I smirk to myself, my heart beating like crazy. Finally, we are closer to discovering what happened and who killed that poor girl.

I jump into the car and enjoy the sound of him stepping on the gas pedal and taking us in the direction of Shawn's place.

Chapter Twenty

Jesse

We reach the address quickly, mostly because I drive like a maniac. The streets are empty, devoid of any people and traffic. After all, it is three in the morning.

Shawn lives on the outskirts of the city. I've been here a couple of times to pick up Bobby, but never really went inside. Never had any need or desire to. Not until now.

Grace and I get out of the car, and we both look at the house. It's actually more of a cottage style house, peaceful and isolated. Isolated being the accent here. There are no other houses nearby, and I wondered a few times why he'd want to live without anyone around. Sometimes, I could understand, but he has no wife or girlfriend who lives with him, so he's all alone. Living isolated with a partner who shares your ideas is great. Living all alone, maybe not so much.

"The lights are all off," Grace tells me, bringing me back to the present moment.

"They would be, right?" I ask. "It's the middle of the night."

"Oh, right," she smiles. I smile back, so she wouldn't think that I meant anything bad by it.

"Let's hope there's someone home, so we can sort this out right here," I say, inhaling deeply and walking over to the door.

I knock on the door, but there is no answer. I turn to her, waiting for some suggestion, but she doesn't say anything. I wait for a few moments, then try knocking again. Still, the result is the same. No response.

Without even thinking, I try the handle, but it's locked.

I glance at the windows. There is no motion inside, no light. Nothing. The place seems empty.

Grace walks up to me and leans closer to my ear. "Maybe try the back?"

Good idea, I think to myself. I smile at her, nodding, then pointing in the direction where we are heading.

We look around, trying to see if there is another way in, or at least if maybe we can be sure that the place is really empty without breaking and entering. Although, I suppose it doesn't matter in the grand scheme of things.

There is no car around. I know that Shawn drives. But that doesn't have to mean anything. We keep walking around the house. There is no cellar, no back door. Just the windows. The sense of unease is palpable. I can almost feel like someone is watching us, but I know that's impossible. I would have seen them.

We make a full circle and find ourselves in front of the door once again. Grace sighs heavily placing her hands on her hips.

"Looks like no one's home," she points out.

"Looks like it, yeah," I nod.

She shakes her head. "Or someone just wants us to think that."

"That's also possible," I agree.

"We have to get in," she says simply, looking at the house. "It doesn't look big. We could search the place in a couple of minutes and make sure he's not here."

"Add breaking and entering to the charges?" I ask, grinning.

"If you're gonna be bad, be bad all the way," she teases, although we both know that I have nothing against doing this.

"Do you like me bad?" I ask, playfully.

I can't believe we chose this moment to flirt, but sometimes, it is out of your hands.

"I like you any way," she beams at me, then quickly regains composure. "But right now, I think we need to focus on the house and that window in the back."

"Which one?" I ask.

She takes me behind and shows me which one. I notice that it's slightly opened. An oversight on the part of the owner, and our good luck.

"I could squeeze my arm through and make it open all the way, if possible," she explains. "I know the drill."

"You know how to break into people's places through the window?" I ask, amused. How many more things are there that I don't know about this girl?

"No, no," she chuckles, trying to keep her voice down. "I meant, I know this type of window. If you press the right button, the opening switches and it's easy to move around, unlike those old windows."

"So, easy to open and without any safety at all," I remark. "Great. I won't be getting any of these new windows then."

"Just give me a boost, will you?" she asks, still smiling.

I stand against the wall, helping her up. I have my hands and fingers linked together, and she steps onto them, holding onto my shoulder and head for balance. She slides her arm inside, and after some careful maneuvering, she manages to do it.

"There," she whispers, pushing the window open.

Before I can tell her to come down so I can go inside first, she jumps in through the window. I rush up after her, falling onto a soft carpet. I get up quickly, looking around. There is nothing but silence around. It really looks like there's no one here.

She walks into the adjacent room, and I rush after her, not wanting to leave her alone. It is the kitchen, also devoid of any presence. We move through the bedroom and living room and are only then convinced that there isn't anyone here.

"Now what?" she asks.

My fists are itching to do some talking, but not the usual kind. It is becoming more and more difficult to control my rage. The very thought that Shawn was the guy who orchestrated all of this makes my stomach clench with anger.

"We talk to the only guy who might know where Shawn is," I say, as I head out the front door.

"What are you doing?" she asks, gasping.

I unlock the door from the inside, because the lock allows me to. Then, I turn to her. "If he comes back, I want him to know that someone was here. I want him to know that I was here. I want him to feel that uneasiness of not knowing what will happen next."

I expect her to say something to that, but she is quiet. I can see understanding in her eyes. She runs to me and together, we walk out of the house, leaving it unlocked. We go to the car, and head over to my brother's place.

"Shouldn't we call first?" Grace wonders. "Maybe your brother is sleeping."

"Maybe Shawn is there, and I don't want to warn him. You know that Bobby isn't good at lying. Shawn will read him immediately." I pause, and a million horrible things pass through my mind, all at the same time. I try to banish them, but it's hard. "That might put Bobby in danger."

"Do you think Shawn would hurt Bobby?" she asks.

"I don't know, and I don't want to risk finding out," I admit, as I step on the gas pedal even harder.

I want to be there as soon as possible. I want to bring this to an end and finally clear my name, by proving that someone else did all of this. Maybe Shawn had nothing to do with Lucy's death, but Grace is right. It is too much of a coincidence.

"You never know with such people," I continue, keeping my eyes focused on the road in front of us. "I really can't believe this..."

It is difficult to process all of this, and I know I have to control myself when I see Shawn, not to grab him by the throat immediately. I have to remain focused. I have to get him to confess, otherwise I have nothing. I know what Jonathan said. It all looks legit. That is the worst thing. It will take me a lot of time and effort to prove anything, so if I want it done as quickly and effectively as possible, I have to get him to confess to everything. And I need witnesses for it.

Grace will be a good witness. If Bobby is there, he will be a good one as well.

I drive faster than usual, because I can't wait to reach Bobby's place. I know they sometimes stay over at each other's house, so I'm hoping this time that is the case as well.

When we're finally there, I rush out of the car but before I can enter the building which I have the keys to, Grace grabs me by the elbow.

"Promise me you'll be careful," she says tenderly.

I can see the love in her eyes. I can see it; I can almost feel it in her words. But I can't say anything to that right now. I can tell her how I feel only after I've cleared my name and shown her that I am not who she thought I was. That I am the man she deserves.

"Can't I get you to stay outside?" I ask again, although I'm sure I will receive the same response as before.

"No way," she shakes her head. "I want to be there. I want to help."

"What if something happens?" I ask, not even wanting to clarify what.

"Let it happen," she tells me. "I want to be by your side, in thick and thin."

I grin. "Are you hinting that you want to marry me?"

She rolls her eyes, letting go of me. "Enough of that," she says. "Let's take care of the important things first, then we'll talk nonsense."

"Deal," I grin, and without even thinking about it, I lean over to give her a peck on the lips. It startles her, but she regains composure quickly, smiling at me.

We climb up the stairs and stop in front of the door which states Bobby's full name. The moment I lift my hand to ring the bell, despite having a key, there is laughter heard from inside, which means Bobby isn't alone.

Impatiently, I ring the doorbell and I wait.

The laughter inside dies. Footsteps are heard, walking over to the door, which opens immediately. Bobby's surprised face greets us both.

"Jesse?" he says my name, then Grace's as well, the moment his eyes befall her face. "Grace? What are you guys doing here?"

Up until this moment, I thought I would control myself. I thought I would explain everything in words and wait for the right time to reveal everything. But that is not what happens. Instead, I push past Bobby.

"Where is he?" I demand to know, entering the living room area like a typhoon.

Shawn jumps up from his seat, not expecting to see me there. I can see the shock on his face, then it all reverts back to the usual.

"Hey, Jesse," he greets me with a smile.

When he sees Grace, he gazes at her incredulously. It takes him a few seconds to realize why we are here... together.

The look on his face is priceless. Only poor Bobby doesn't seem to get what's going on, but the three of us do.

"You fucking asshole," I growl at him, with Grace holding me by the elbow. "You'll pay for what you did!"

Bobby eyes us all in disbelief, finally speaking up. "Will someone tell me what the heck is going on?"

Chapter Twenty-One

Grace

"Why don't you ask your best buddy there what the heck is going on," Jesse says in an angry voice. "Because I've been wondering that myself for the past two weeks."

Bobby turns to Shawn, his baby blue eyes wide with surprise that anything could have been happening behind his back between his brother and his best friend. I watch the trio clash, as I know that I'm only here as a silent bystander. Whatever needs to happen will happen between Shawn and Jesse. Bobby and I are irrelevant here.

"What's going on, Shawn?" Bobby asks, almost pleading.

Shawn looks over at Jesse. I can immediately tell that Jesse is barely controlling himself from pouncing on Shawn, and the only reason he hasn't done that yet is because he's trying to get everything out in the open.

"I don't know," Shawn says, sounding confused. "What are you talking about, Jesse?"

Jesse instantly tries to lunge at him, but I manage to keep him from doing so. Shawn jerks backward, trying to increase the distance between him and Jesse.

"Tell him how you've been stealing money from my company!" Jesse hisses at him venomously.

"Shawn?" Bobby gasps, turning to his best friend. "Is that true?"

"Tell him!" Jesse demands, and I know everyone is on the verge of breaking. It won't end well.

"That's a lie!" Shawn shouts back. "How dare you accuse me of something like that!"

"It's not a lie and you know it, you bastard!" Jesse howls back at him, and it sounds like they're having a shouting contest, trying to outdo the other. "I have proof! You can't keep lying your way out of this! The only reason I haven't called the cops yet is because I want to hear you say it, you piece of shit!"

Shawn doesn't say anything to that. Immediately upon hearing Jesse's words that he's got proof, the expression on Shawn's face changes. His usually reddish cheeks have now turned pale, and his eyes are as wide as bicycle wheels. All eyes are on him, waiting to hear what he will say to this.

I dare not comment, and I see that Bobby is in the same boat. We exchanged a meaningful glance a moment ago, but now, we're all staring at Shawn. He has to admit. He just has to. Otherwise, I'm not sure I can control Jesse any longer, and God knows what might happen then.

Shawn's face takes on a whole new expression. His eyes narrow, growing darker somehow, as hatred shoots out of every look he sends in Jesse's direction.

"You always thought you were such a fuckin' hot shot," Shawn finally starts speaking, and his voice is deep and dark, not at all aligned with his outer persona. It's like someone else is speaking from inside of him. "But you're not," he adds. "You're nothing. Someone had to prove this to you."

"And that someone had to be you?" Jesse snorted.

"Shawn... why?" Bobby interrupted, unable to keep quiet. I could see the pain of betrayal on his face.

"And you," Shawn turned to him, with a disgusted expression. "You've always been in his shadow. Why?"

"That's not true," Bobby says, faltering.

"It fucking is," Shawn grimaces at him. "You don't even have the balls to admit it. I had to do something about it."

"So, you decided to steal money from my company," Jesse snarled. "The company that gives you your paycheck."

"I could have gotten a job anywhere else, you conceited asshole," Shawn replies irritably. "The only reason I agreed to work for you was to be able to do this."

"Did you really think you'd get away with it?" Jesse asks, shaking his head.

Shawn shrugs. "Nothing points to me. Not about the theft or about the girl."

"The girl??" Bobby sounds shocked, his hand pressing his chest. He looks like he's about to pass out. "Shawn, you didn't..."

"He did," Jesse nods. "Grace was right. She said it's too much of a coincidence to have those two things happen at the same time, revolving around me. She suggested that the same person did it, and now, it turns out, she was right."

This time, Shawn looks in my direction. His gaze is trying to intimidate me, but I know he can't hurt me, not with Jesse and Bobby around. But he's still trying to send me those hateful glares.

"Admit it," Jesse demands.

Shawn scoffs at him. "Why? So, you'll feel better about yourself?"

"This has nothing to do with me, you piece of shit!" Jesse is beyond himself with rage. "It has everything to do with Lucy Romero. Why would you hurt her? What had she done to deserve that?"

Shawn frowns before he replies. "The bitch found out I was stealing money from the company. I don't know how. She must have overheard me talking to the guy at the bank. Then, she approached me and told me if I didn't give her a cut, she'd come to you and tell you all about it. I'm not that stupid. I know she would have milked me dry of all she could, then she would either go to the cops and make a deal for herself, or she would have gone straight to you. I had to get rid of her if I wanted this to work. Then, the cherry on top was the idea to pin the murder on you. I'd have your money and you'd be behind bars. Poetic justice, don't you think?"

"Poetic my ass!" Jesse snarls at him, and at that moment, I can't do anything to hold him back.

He lunges straight at Shawn. Bobby and I gasp, unable to control the situation. Everything is now between these two men, fighting.

They both fall to the ground, rolling, snarling at each other. Jesse punches him in the face with his fist, but that doesn't do much to Shawn. He is foaming at the mouth, with a crazed look in his eyes.

They roll again, and Jesse is on top of him, his hands around the man's neck, squeezing tight.

"Don't kill him!" Bobby shouts, but he does nothing. He knows he can't go against his brother, just like he can't believe that his best friend isn't who he thought he was.

We both watch the sight before our eyes unfurling. Shawn first grips Jesse's hands, but then his arms fly around him. Somehow, he finds the strength to push Jesse off of himself. There are more blows dealt on both ends.

"We have to stop this!" Bobby turns to me, and I know he's right.

"Call the police!" I tell him, rushing to try and separate the two men.

Shawn punches Jesse on the jaw. I grab him by the arm when he aims at Jesse again, preventing him from dealing another blow.

"You bitch!" Shawn turns to me, slapping me on the cheek so hard that I stumble backwards against the wall. I press my cold palm to my burning cheek. There is little pain. Only a horrible stinging sensation that slowly finds its way up to the back of my neck, exploding into a headache.

Jesse is up again. His lip is cracked. There is a trickle of blood dripping down the corner of his mouth. He spits angrily to the side. Without waiting, he rushes at Shawn, and this time, they both stumble down against a nearby coffee table. A glass lamp falls down to the ground, breaking into several big pieces.

It all then happens in the blink of an eye. A flash of glass and then, blood starts to trickle onto the floor.

At first, I'm not even sure whose blood it is. You always assume that it's the other guy who's hurt, never the one you're rooting for. But on second glance, I realize to my shock that it is Jesse who's bleeding.

He's bent over, his hand pressing to his side. His hand bloody. And the blood won't stop flowing.

Shawn stands up before him, with a large, knife-like piece of glass in his hand. Blood is dripping from it in small droplets, making another puddle on the floor.

I can't breathe. Everything stops. The world isn't turning anymore. We're all frozen in time and space.

I'm not even aware of what I'm doing. Shawn raises the glass again. I know what he's about to do. He wants to hurt Jesse. No. He wants to kill him. I have to do something.

I look around frantically. I notice a bookshelf. There is a row of encyclopedias. I rush for it, grabbing the biggest, heaviest, hardcovered one. It's beyond heavy. I lift it up as high as I can, then I swing it at Shawn, hitting him straight over the head. A loud thump noise is heard and without another word, Shawn slumps down onto the ground, like a lifeless puppet.

"Shawn!" Bobby shouts, rushing over to him.

I run to Jesse instead. I put his head into my lap, keeping him awake. We're both pressing on his wound. We have to stop the bleeding until the cops and the ambulance come.

I turn to Bobby. "Did you call the cops!?" I shout at him. He nods, frightened, completely frozen. "Now call the ambulance!"

The sound of my voice is enough to bring him back to reality. I watch him grab his phone and dial the ambulance. He manages to tell them what happened in short, and the address.

"They're coming in ten minutes," he tells me, stumbling over letters as if he's just learned to speak properly and needs more practice.

I look down at Jesse. His eyes are barely open. I slap him on the cheek, and this makes him wide awake again.

"That..." he starts, his voice low and weak. "Fucking... hurts..."

"The slap or the wound?" I ask.

He grins. "Both."

I smile. "Since you're able to make jokes, smart ass, you won't be dying."

"I could..." he starts, but coughs. "Still surprise... you."

"I want you to surprise me," I nod, still smiling at him. "But minus the blood, please."

"Deal..." he manages to muster, closing his eyes.

"No, no, no," I shake him a little. "Stay with me. You have to stay awake. Just ten minutes, you hear?"

My voice luckily keeps him awake. But he's the smartass he's always been.

"Not so... loud," he says. "Sleepy."

"You can sleep in the hospital," I tell him. "When they do whatever they need to do to make sure you're alright. But for now, I need you to stay with me."

"I love you," he suddenly says, without faltering this time.

"No, no," I shake my head. "You're only saying it now because you think you're dying. I'm only accepting it if you say it, and everything is alright."

He grins again. "Tough... crowd."

"The toughest," I nod, caressing his cheek.

I don't dare look down at his wound. I can feel the warm wetness seeping through my fingers. I press harder, but I know that's not enough. Where is that fucking ambulance??

At that moment, Bobby comes over. He's trembling.

"Is he OK?" he asks, staring at his brother.

"He will be," I assure him. "Just keep him awake. That's what we need to do right now."

Suddenly, someone barges in through the door.

"Police!" Someone in the hallway shouts.

Relief washes over me. I glance in Shawn's direction. He's still lying lifeless on the floor. I have no idea how hard I hit him. To be honest, I don't care. All I care about is the man whose oozing blood before me. He is the only one I want to save.

But when I look down, I realize he's closed his eyes.

"Jesse!" I shout, trying to wake him, but he's not responsive. "Jesse, please wake up, please!"

My echoes fill the room, and fear grips my heart stronger than ever. The thought of losing him is too much to handle. It all becomes a haze of terror and I barely even hear the sound of the paramedics telling me to move away, so they can help him.

Chapter Twenty-Two

Jesse

When I open my eyes, a shimmering white light attacks my retinas. I close them quickly, blinking heavily. My entire body is in pain and I don't feel it in just one place. It's like there is pain in every bloodstream, every part of my body, just continuing to spread around.

I try to open my eyes again. This time, it is slightly better, although that whiteness is still too bright. I blink a few more times, allowing my eyes to adjust to the surroundings. I recognize the beeping noise immediately. I don't even need to turn around to know that there is a machine, and it is somehow connected to my body.

I recognize everything else. It is a hospital room. The same kind I've never been in but the one I've seen in movies and TV shows. I try to prop myself up on the bed, but a sudden and quite unexpected sharp pain cuts right through me. That same pain brings back the memory of what happened.

I was stabbed.

The sentence forms inside my mind so suddenly that I barely believe it. But the pain assures me it's true.

I finally manage to lift myself a bit in bed. Just a small exertion and I immediately feel like I've run a whole marathon. My heart beats faster. My breathing becomes quicker, more shallow. I try to steady it, because the steadier my breathing is, the lighter the pain is.

I look around. I'm alone in the room. I wonder where everyone is. Grace should be here. Bobby, too.

I remember how she smacked Shawn over the head with a book. A book, of all things!

The thought makes me grin to myself, like a madman thinking of crazy ideas and plans. But it's not a crazy idea or a plan. It's the mere knowledge of knowing that she feels the same way about me as I do about her.

At that moment, the door opens and Bobby walks in. He's holding a plastic cup in his hand. The moment he sees me, he almost drops it to the ground.

"Jesse!" he shouts. "You're awake!"

"Barely," I smile. "But let's go with yours."

He sits down carefully on the bed next to me, taking me by the hand. "How do you feel?"

"Like I've been stabbed," I reply. "It's no fun."

Bobby smiles, but it's an apprehensive smile. I can immediately tell.

"What about... Shawn?" I ask.

That apprehensiveness immediately transforms into rage. "He survived, if that's what you mean."

"Grace smashed a book on his head?" I ask, grinning still.

"Yeah," he smiles this time, a real smile. Then, that smile dies out. It gets extinguished, like a candle in the wind. "She acted. I... I froze."

I realize now why all that apprehension. He thinks he is to blame for this. He thinks he should have acted, but the truth is that such a situation makes you freeze. You just don't know what to do, because you don't know which side you should turn to. I want him to know that I understand.

"I'm glad he's not dead," I say, and I mean it.

"Really?" Bobby seems surprised.

"Sure," I nod. "I want him to rot in prison for what he did to Lucy. If it's really true that she tried to blackmail him into sharing that money, that still doesn't mean that she deserved the fate that she got."

Bobby just nods. "At least her family has closure now, thanks to you and Grace."

"I wouldn't have been able to do this without her, you know."

"I should have been the one to help you," Bobby says apologetically. "I was supposed to be the one to reveal all of this with you, but I wasn't. Shawn was my best friend and I never– "

"I know," I interrupt him.

I know exactly what he wants to say. I know how hard it must be for him to say it, so I want to save him the heartache. Not that it matters anymore. Everything is finally finished.

"I don't think I've been living in your shadow all my life," he continues, and I realize this is something that he needs to get off his chest. So, I let him. "You've always been my big brother, and big brothers are supposed to look out for their younger siblings. That is what I always thought our relationship was like. You took care of me, like brothers should. On my part, there has never been any envy or jealousy. When your company took off, I was glad for you. I was even more proud to call you my brother. There has never been anything but love in my heart for you."

"I know that," I smile back, touched by this sudden outburst of emotion.

But I realize that we've never spoken to each other like this. We always shared a silent brotherly bond, one that did not require either side to say those three words aloud for us to know that was exactly how we felt.

"I wanted you to have everything I had," I assure him. "None of this would have made me happy otherwise."

"But it's me who brought Shawn into our lives," he suddenly says. "I remember how he used to talk so highly of you, but little by little, that changed. He would talk against you, and I see now that he wanted us to turn against each other."

"He didn't manage to do that," I remind him. "No one would ever be able to do it. That is probably why he resorted to that horrible thing he did. I don't care about the money. You can always make more. But taking a human life... that is something you can never wash away from your soul."

Bobby nods pensively. I know he's wondering what will now happen to Shawn. To be honest, I don't care. All I care about is that girl's family getting closure. Also, my name being cleared. There is no longer a stain on it. I don't have the fear of ending up in prison for something I haven't done.

"As for Grace..." I start, realizing that I haven't mentioned anything about her yet. He doesn't know that we've gotten close, much closer than either of us intended to get, I think.

"There is no need to explain anything," he tells me, with a knowledgeable smile. "The instant you guys appeared in front of my door together, I picked up on what's been going on between you two."

"Is it that obvious?" I grin.

"Only to someone who really knows you," he explains.

I've always heard of that cliché, that love makes you glow, it makes you smile all the time and that sort of stuff. But I never really believed it. I always believed that you make your own happiness, just like you make your own sadness. No one can infect you with either of those two things.

However, now some things seem much clearer. It's not that some people can create happiness for you, but they are an active participant in it. A crucial ingredient, sort of. That is what Grace is. A crucial ingredient in my happiness, and no matter how hard I've been trying to fight it, I have to surrender at this point. It is useless to keep fighting.

"And..." I hesitate to ask my next question. "Is that alright with you?"

Only now has that thought occurred to me. I felt as if I've completely forgotten that my brother dated Grace as well, and that maybe, just maybe, he might have some feelings for her still. The last thing I want to do is live my happy life at the expense of my brother's own happiness.

He gives me a reassuring smile. "It is more than alright," he says. "What we had was in the past. When we broke up, there was a time I might have thought that could have been a mistake, but slowly, I came to realize that we were simply not meant for each other. We're both good people, but we're just not good enough for each other."

"You don't know how happy that makes me," I admit. "Because I was afraid that this might come between us."

"Never," he assures me. "We're brothers forever. And to tell you honestly, I met someone a few weeks back, someone I've taken out for coffee a few times. It's just that with all of this happening, I didn't get the chance to mention it yet."

My eyebrows raise at him curiously. "What's her name?"

"Jennie," he says. "She is the sweetest thing ever."

"If you say so, I'm sure she is," I nod. "Maybe we could all go out for a double date, once I'm feeling better... unless, of course you think it might be awkward."

"Why?" he shrugs. "Why bring something from the past to you in the present? Leave it there. Grace is a lovely girl, but I have no feelings for her anymore, just like I'm sure she doesn't have any feelings for me."

"You're right," I agree. "You know what? I've learned something very important from all this."

"What is that?" he asks, sounding amused.

"The past should be left in the past," I note. "And never judge a book by its cover. That, too," I chuckle.

He laughs as well. After everything that's happened, it feels so good to know that the burden of potential guilt has been lifted off my shoulders, and I can live again, truly live, without any fear. That is also the lesson I've learned.

Right then, a knock on the door is heard. We both look in that direction. The door opens, and Grace peers through. Her green eyes widen in surprise when she sees me awake.

"Jesse!" she squeals in delight, rushing over to me and wrapping her arms around me, to bring us as close as we can be. I close my eyes, inhaling her scent, as her fiery red hair cascades all around us. I love it when she leaves it loose, like a river of fire.

I can't help but grin at this outburst of emotion. Bobby watches us for a moment, then he heads out.

"I'll give you guys some privacy," he smiles, closing the door behind him.

She pulls away from me, looking at me lovingly, with so much devotion.

"Now, you can repeat what you told me a few hours ago," she says with a mischievous grin on those beautiful lips.

Chapter Twenty-Three

Grace

"What did I say?" he asks, teasing me with those eyes of his. "You have to remind me."

"You nearly died, and you're still being a smartass," I roll my eyes at him playfully. "Seriously?"

"I have partial amnesia," he continues along the same lines, and it's becoming more and more difficult not to laugh. "I only remember certain things from last night, like the one I almost died. Now, as for what I did exactly or what I said, you have to help me with that one."

"That's very clever," I chuckle loudly this time, taking him by the hand.

"Remind me," he says. "Please."

"Well, seeing you're asking so nicely," I nod, my heart feeling as if it's about to burst out of my chest.

I take a deep breath, watching him. I clear my throat a little, trying to shake off the nerves that are about to wash over me. The moment has come. Neither of us can keep these feelings bottled up inside any longer. Even if he was talking nonsense and he didn't mean what he said, I have to know, for my own peace of mind.

I expect his eyes to be blurry and confused, but they are looking at me with expectation and hope. I see in them a reflection of my own eyes, my own emotions.

"You said you loved me," I finally muster the courage to say those words, my voice barely above a whisper.

Then, he does something I'm not expecting him to. He frowns. He doesn't look like he's in agreement with this. My heart clenches heavily. Is it possible that he really doesn't remember saying it?

"Did I?" he asks, wondering.

"Mhm," I nod, feeling my heart drop down into a deep, dark chasm and I doubt it will come out to the surface soon.

The way he frowns makes me want to let go of his hand, turn around and run out of this room. The weight of my confession is pressing heavily upon me, but I have to stay until the end, even if the confession isn't what I expect it to be.

"You did," I say again, trying to gather more courage, which is seeping away from me.

"I don't recall saying it like that," he corrects me, bringing my hand to his lips and kissing it softly. "I think I said I love you, not I loved you."

I immediately realize what he's trying to do. Without thinking, I punch him playfully on the shoulder.

"You asshole!" I shout, unable to stop laughing, but at the same time, feeling that onslaught of nerves calm down little by little.

"Ouch!" he shouts back, also laughing. "You could be a little more careful, you know. I've just been stabbed."

"Then stop teasing me," I pretend to pout.

"I love you," he says again. I can hear his voice trembling, even more than mine. "I think I always did. I think all that antagonism stemmed from that very fact. You were my brother's girlfriend, and I wanted you to be mine instead. I could not rectify those two things, and it resulted in the way I treated you. I was wrong, Grace. I am so sorry for assuming things, for not seeing you the way you deserved to be seen. But I see you now. I see you and I love you."

For a moment, there is only silence in the room. My heart is pounding in my chest, as my mind struggles to process all the words he's just said.

"I love you, too, Jesse," I tell him.

I lean closer to him and press my lips to his. I feel the joy of relief flooding throughout my entire body. I close my eyes, giving all of myself to this moment, losing myself in this kiss, in the soft touch of his lips. Finally, things are as they should be. Only... one more thing needs to be clarified.

I pull away suddenly and unexpectedly.

"What is it?" he asks, immediately recognizing the confusion in my eyes.

"There is something else," I say, biting my lower lip. "Something I should have told you earlier, but I couldn't."

"What is it?" he wonders. "You can tell me anything. Unless it's the fact that you were just pulling my leg about loving me back. I'm not accepting that."

I chuckle, grateful at his effort for trying to alleviate the situation.

"When we went to the villa to look for clues," I start, wanting to choose my words carefully, to explain everything, but instead, words just flow out of me. "I found a cigarette on the floor in the kitchen."

"You did?" he asks, sounding surprised. "You didn't tell me."

"No," I admit. "I put it in my pocket. I... I didn't want to show you."

"Why not?" he wonders. "You didn't believe me?"

"No, no, it's not that," I shake my head at him. "I didn't want anyone else to find it. Because I knew that if they did, that might be proof of you being there at a later time than when you stated. Also, I didn't want you to worry about it. You already had enough on your mind. I wanted to keep hold of it, so no one would find it. It's actually still in my apartment."

"Why didn't you throw it away?" he asks.

"I thought maybe there is someone else's DNA on it," I explain. "If worse came to worst, I would have shown it to my boss, but only if I was sure that it will be proof of your innocence and not your guilt."

"So... you had my back?" he asks, clarifying. The sound of his voice is already changed back to the way it was a moment ago.

"Always," I nod. "From the moment you entered my boss' office."

"I wasn't very nice then, was I?" he admits.

"You were the suspect for a murder you didn't do," I remind him. "We can cut you some slack for being rude."

"Gee, thanks," he grins, and we both laugh together.

"So, how long do you need to stay at the hospital?" I ask.

"The doc said eight days," he tells me. "Then, I can go home."

I think about it for a moment. "But... who will take care of you?"

He tries to shrug, but obviously it's painful, because his facial expression changes and he frowns. "I should remember not to do that for a while. Well, I can take care of myself, you know... unless, maybe you and Titi want to be my roommates for a month or so, until I feel well enough."

I pretend to ponder, patting my chin with the tip of my index finger. "I have a problem with that." I decide to tease him as well, just like he teased me about his love confession.

"What problem?" he asks seriously.

A beeping noise of the machine next to his bed interrupts my train of thought, but I manage to capture it again.

"What if Titi and I like it at your place so much that we want to stay there forever and ever?" I ask playfully.

"Hmmm." Now, he starts patting his chin, mirroring my actions. "That is quite a problem."

"See?" I point out, suppressing a bout of laughter. "Maybe it's best for us not to come at all."

"No, no, no," he shakes his head. "It's settled."

"It is?" I ask, pretending I'm not sure.

He pulls me closer to him, despite the pain that this effort awakens in him. We're staring into each other's eyes, and I know that in him, I've finally found my happily ever after, without even looking for it.

"I never want you to leave my side again," he tells me.

"I never will," I smile.

Just as we're about to kiss again, a nurse opens the door. She seems to immediately recognize that she interrupted a tender moment.

"I apologize, but visiting hours are over," she informs us both.

"I'll be right out," I assure her. "Thank you."

She acknowledges my reply with a nod, then leaves us alone for a minute more.

"Going home?" he asks.

"Mhm," I agree. "I need a shower."

"Lemme see," he says, smelling my neck. "Nah. You're good. You smell delicious."

"Don't be silly," I chuckle. "I'll go home, but I'll be here in the morning, if they let me see you."

"Start packing," he reminds me. "I would have given you my key now, but I have no idea what they did to my belongings."

"Your key?" I echo.

"Is it too fast?" he wonders, sounding almost apologetic.

"No, no," I shake my head, smiling. "It's... just right. Everything about this is just right."

"Well then, my Goldilocks," he chuckles. "Go home and rest. Pet that sweet cat of yours for me."

"Oh, yes... Titi," I suddenly remember. "You won't mind if I bring her with me?"

"Mind?" He tilts his head as he speaks. "I'm actually into the cat, but I can't very well take her away from you, and just keep her without you. Right?"

"Right," I laugh. "We're a pair. You can't separate us."

"And I wouldn't have it any other way," he smiles at me, his words sinking to the bottom of my heart, where they would remain forever more.

Bobby takes me home, and although I initially think it'll be an awkward drive, it's not. We do a recap of what happened, and how he feels guilty that he didn't see what was right in front of his face.

"Don't blame yourself," I tell him, the moment he parks the car in front of my apartment building. "You couldn't have known. Obviously, the man is a psychopath. They're very good at pretending to be normal people."

"Yeah," he replies, but he still doesn't sound convinced.

"Just... choose better friends from now on," I tease.

He smiles. "I will. And also, you and Jesse... I'm really glad for you guys."

I pause for a moment, trying to see if there is any underlying message in his statement, but there's nothing. Bobby has always been this nice guy who wanted the best for everyone. Only, we don't live in a world where this is possible. There will always be those who are unhappy, who are envious and jealous. These things are inevitable. All we can do is make sure we're not one of those people.

"Thank you," I reply. "That really means a lot."

"And also... I'm sorry I didn't handle our breakup very... well, very nicely."

I smile, appreciating the gesture. "Thanks. That really means a lot, although it's all water under the bridge."

With those words, I wrap my arms around him, and he hugs me back. There is nothing romantic about it, just pure joy that everything is finally as it should be. I wish him goodnight, and two hours later, I'm sitting on the sofa, with Titi purring at my feet.

I wouldn't be able to fall asleep even if I tried. I never thought I'd say something like this, but with me and Jesse, it's a tale as old as time. If someone told me that he would be the soul to complete my own, I'd tell them they were crazy. But here we are, completing each other, complementing each other, and through hardship, growing together, overcoming all the obstacles in our way.

Titi stirs a little in her sleep. I lean down to pet her on the head. She opens her eyes but only for a single moment. Then, she dozes off again.

I don't know when it is that I close my eyes, but sleep takes over me and I let go. Everything is alright with the world. The fact that in just a few days, I will be waking up and falling asleep in Jesse's bed next to him is something I never thought would happen. Now, it seems the most wonderous thing in the world, and I can't wait for it.

Chapter Twenty-Four

Jesse

Only three months have passed since those fateful events, but I knew that there was no point in waiting. Why wait, when you are absolutely certain that this is it?

Those are my thoughts on that pleasantly warm August afternoon. The breeze is blowing through the trees. The sun is shining warmly, although not scorchingly. Everything is pure perfection. There are just a dozen guests. No more are necessary. We both agreed that we wanted something small, something intimate.

However, what I wasn't expecting was for Grace to ask to have it here, of all places.

I have to admit that Bobby and his girlfriend, who is an interior decorator, did a great job making this place as beautiful as ever. There are purple and white flowers everywhere, and the tables are decorated with white linen, adorned with candles on top. Soft, romantic music is playing in the background. When I look around, I feel blessed that there are all these people who love and support us.

But Grace... she is the sun after a storm. Knowing what I do now, it is painfully obvious that I wouldn't have done it without her. Everything I am now I owe to her.

"Are you ready?" Bobby asks, standing by my side. He adjusts my bow tie a little, and smiles. "Lookin' great."

"I've never been more ready," I say, listening to the sound of the music that will announce Grace's walk down the aisle.

There it is. We all turn to face her. She is walking with her mother, as she said she would. She had lost her father a few years back, but she didn't want to do this on her own. She wanted to hold her mother by the hand, and I said I thought that was a great idea. Now, seeing them both like that, I know I haven't made a mistake in agreeing to it.

Grace is wearing a stunning white dress, which is accentuating her curves to perfection. In her hand, there is a bouquet of white and purple flowers. My heart skips a beat at seeing her standing by my side and offering to take me by the hand, which I immediately do.

"You look breathtaking," I lean over to tell her.

She smiles, blushing. "Thank you."

I'm unable to take my eyes off her. I can't believe that I'm about to marry the woman of my dreams, the woman who stuck by my side when no one else would, who believed in my innocence when all evidence pointed otherwise. The tidal wave of emotion washes over me, and I allow myself to drown in it.

We exchange our vows and then our rings in a heartfelt ceremony, and then seal our union with a kiss. Everyone starts clapping and cheering. When I pull away from her, she is smiling. That smile is making me feel like I'm on top of the world.

Our first dance is a song she chose. I honestly couldn't care less about the song, as long as I have her in my arms to dance with, for the rest of our lives.

We move slowly to the rhythm of the music. She allows me to lead.

"I can't believe we're married," she suddenly tells me, as her hand melts into mine. "It feels like a dream come true."

"I know," I agree, smiling. "I feel the same way."

"I lost all hope that I would find my happily ever after," she admits.

"But... why?" I ask.

"There has been too much heartache in my life," she shrugs, allowing me to spin her as the music continues. "I wanted to shield my heart, and then you came along."

"And ruined everything," I chuckle.

"Exactly," she laughs. "I never thought I would say this, but you are my perfect match, my soulmate."

"I will love you for the rest of my life," I tell her, feeling overwhelmed by all the emotions and my inability to control them.

The music stops and so do we. She leans over to me and kisses me, and we are awarded yet another applause. We look around, accepting everyone's congratulations. Then, as the afternoon continues, the guests all start to dance and enjoy the festivities.

By the time the wedding celebration comes to an end, some of the guests decide to go back home, while most of them stay at the villa. Bidding most of them goodnight, Grace and I hide away in the main bedroom.

She walks over to the big window, which stretches from the ceiling all the way to the floor. It overlooks the mountain opposite us, but in the darkness, barely anything is visible. Nonetheless, she stands in front of the window, gazing outward.

I walk over behind her, wrapping my arms around her waist. The moon is casting a soft glow over the mountain, not enough to illuminate much, but enough to see faint outlines of nature sprawled before us. I pull her closer, resting my chin on her shoulder.

"Are you sorry that we had the wedding here?" I ask.

"Never," she shakes her head. "This is a beautiful place."

"Even with knowing what happened here?" I ask, hesitantly. "We could still sell it, you know."

I said I would sell the place. I said I didn't want anything to do with it once I was cleared of all accusations. But then, she surprised me with her wish: she wanted to have the wedding here, at the villa where the murder of Lucy Romero happened.

I have to admit that I was shocked. I wasn't expecting her to say anything like that. I thought she would agree with me, to just sell the place, get a new one and make it into our new home. She said something completely different. She wanted to keep this place, and in a way, see it reborn. I asked her to clarify. She immediately did so. She said that she wanted to breathe new life into this wonderful house. That such a place did not deserve the fate of a ghost house, but rather the fate of a family house.

"But... someone died here," I reminded her when we spoke about it. I wanted to see if she truly thought about all of it.

"Someone died on every inch of this earth, inside a building or outside of it," she explained to me, shrugging as if none of that mattered at all. "We're basically walking on graveyards, blood and bones soaked up into the ground. And we don't even think about that."

"That might be so, but we know who died inside my house," I remind her.

"And because we know who died, we know not to be afraid," she points out. "She won't haunt us. We did nothing to her. In fact, we helped unearth her killer. If anything, she should be grateful to us and not haunt our home."

I chuckled at those words when she said them. "OK, OK," I nodded. "You really want us to live here in the villa?"

"Yes, I really do," she said, and that was that.

Now, we find ourselves in that same place, in the bedroom, lost in thought. I want to taste her again. I want to whisper sweet nothings into her ear. I want her to lie down on my chest so she can listen to the soft beating of my heart. But I don't move. I dare not move, as if that action might break the magic of the moment. At this moment, there is nothing else to think about, nothing else to consider but her and her happiness.

"Jesse?" I hear her say, almost whisper.

"What is it, baby?" I ask, overwhelmed by tenderness for this sweet, delicate woman who has given herself to me, to love and honor, to cherish and hold for the rest of our lives.

"I have something to tell you," she says, turning to me.

"What is it?" I ask again, in the same words, as I'm trying to read the expression on her face. She locks her gaze with mine, but I can't see anything in those fathomless eyes other than profound love. I see nothing that would be a cause for concern, and yet, her voice assures me there is apprehension in her words.

"Are you happy?" she asks.

I smile, cupping her chin with my fingers. "Isn't that obvious?"

"I'm asking you, really," she says softly.

"Really," I nod. "You are all I could possibly need."

Suddenly, it seems to me as if I said something wrong. Her forehead knits. She frowns.

"So, you don't want anything to change?"

"Why would I?" I shrug. "This is perfect."

"Oh..." she sighs, looking down at her feet, which are bare now, peeking from underneath her long, white dress.

"Grace," I say her name tenderly. "Talk to me. What is going on? What's with all this questioning? Are you rethinking marrying me?"

Her eyes widen in shock. "What? No, no, absolutely not."

"Then, what is it? What has you so worried?"

"I..." she starts, pressing her hands to her belly. It takes me only a moment to realize what she's saying. "I'm pregnant, Jesse."

Her words echo in the room around us. It takes me a while to process what she just said. She takes it as hesitation, and immediately continues talking, like a wind-up doll, using every single word she can think of to try and explain herself.

"I know we haven't talked about kids yet, and I know it's too soon, but– "

Before she can continue, I grab her by the waist and lift her high up in the air, spinning her about. She giggles loudly, resting her hands on my shoulder for support. It is the most wonderful sound I've ever heard.

"Are you serious?" I ask after putting her down and cupping her face with my hands.

"Yes," she smiles. "Are you... OK with that?"

"OK?" I sound incredulous because I am. "I'm more than OK. I'm ecstatic!"

She seems relieved, and finally, she beams at me with those loving eyes.

"I was so afraid you would say that it's too soon," she admits, biting her lip.

"We haven't talked about it at all," I confess as well. "So, I haven't really been thinking about it, but now that you mention it, the very thought fills me with joy."

"It does?" she gushes.

I press my hands to her belly. "This baby will be so loved."

She wraps her arms around my neck, kissing me on the lips. I can't resist the temptation any longer. I've been meaning to do this since I saw her in this beautiful dress. Our kiss is slow and gentle, filled with passion and love. We both lose ourselves in this moment of sheer bliss, which I know will last forever.

I lift her in my arms and take her to bed. I feel her shivering, and I know it's not from the cold. Her body, just like mine, is overwhelmed. Our desire cannot be sustained any longer. We have to give in.

I put her gently on the bed, adjusting myself on top of it. I lift her dress, spreading her legs. She feels so hot to the touch, like a volcano about to erupt. I feel the same way.

"How did a guy like me get so lucky?" I ask, not having the slightest idea where that question came from.

She caresses me with the palm of her hand. "We both got lucky," she tells me.

Our lips lock again, and my cock becomes harder than ever. I slide into her effortlessly, enjoying the sound of her moaning against my lips.

"I love you, I love you so much..." I tell her, as I thrust deeply into her, her body adjusting itself to take all of me into her.

She wraps her legs around me, keeping me close. She bucks her hips upward. I dive into her, she takes all of me, and it feels like pure bliss.

Her heat envelops me, her pussy clenches around my tight, throbbing cock.

"Forever..." she murmurs against my lips, and we come together at the same time, both of us exploding onto each other, feeling our juices mix together.

As we break apart, we gaze into each other's eyes, our love oozing out of every look, every breath, every touch. Looking at her, I know we're meant to be together. Nothing will ever tear us apart.

We spend the rest of the night wrapped in each other's arms, with her head on my chest. Our hearts beat together, in unison. We are finally content and at peace. We have overcome the most difficult period. Now, we know that we will always have each other and that is all that matters.

We sleep long, until the morning breaks, our bodies intertwined, and our love unbreakable.

Epilogue – Five Years Later

Grace

Having our first baby was a breeze. Emma is the most wonderful, the most curious little four year old I could ever have hoped for. The inquisitive look in her eyes when she sees a bee or a butterfly, or when she does not understand why something falls to the ground instead of flying like a bird, are the moments both Jesse and I love the most.

Eventually, we both agreed that having another child close in age would be perfect. But things don't always go according to plan. While Emma came easily, our second child proves to be somewhat of a struggle. Not to say that doing the baby dance is a boring endeavor. On the contrary. We always try to keep it light and fun, and not a chore that has to provide a certain result.

Still, despite all our efforts, our second, beloved baby will simply not come to us. At least, not until that fateful day, which only strengthens my belief that things always come to you, not when you think you need them the most, but when you actually do. Because sometimes, you don't know what it is exactly you need. Like with Jesse. I had no idea I needed him, and yet, he stumbled into my office that day, and an entire avalanche was started, ending with us together, in our own little happily ever after.

However, we still need one more ingredient to that happily ever after. And that's what never leaves my mind. Not even that afternoon, when we find ourselves strolling through the park.

I know that many people would lose hope after two years of trying. But not us. As long as I have Jesse and Emma by my side, I feel like I should consider myself a lucky woman. And I do. But there is that yearning that wants to be satiated and there is nothing I can do about it.

We stroll through the park, hand in hand. It is one of those rare afternoons that we get solely to each other, because Emma got to spend the afternoon with Uncle Bobby, who took her to the local circus. When he appeared in front of our door with two tickets, she squealed with delight. Usually, she prefers it when we all go together. But little by little, she has become freer with Bobby, and we couldn't have been more happy about that, especially because of the fact that Bobby and his wife are also expecting a child of their own in three months.

When we decided to take a little stroll this afternoon, we had no idea that everything would change. We're enjoying a light banter, this time talking about how they fixed up the park, and the cops being on patrol for the past two years has also cleared up the drug dealer issue.

"Seems like we're making the whole city a better place together," Jesse snickers, watching a few other couples stroll slowly, enjoying their time together.

"Absolutely," I nod, but before I can say anything else, I feel a sudden wave of nausea hit me like a tidal wave.

I stumble lightly, holding onto Jesse for balance. Reacting quickly, he catches my arm to steady me.

"Are you alright?" he asks, concern etched on his handsome face.

I inhale deeply, feeling that pang deep down in my belly. "I'm not sure," I admit. "I just feel a little nauseous, that's all."

"Could it be something you ate?" he asks, sounding worried.

"The pizza?" I wonder. "No way. We always eat there, and I never felt nauseous from their food."

"Do you want to sit down on a bench?" he suggests.

"No," I shake my head. "I'm fine. I really want to walk a little more. I feel like we're stuck inside the house all day long."

We continue to walk, but a few moments later, that same onslaught of nausea happens again. Only this time, it's much worse. I feel a strange fluttering inside my stomach, something familiar that I haven't felt in a long time. I stop walking. Jesse immediately stops with me, looking at me, all puzzled.

"What is it?" he asks.

A sudden realization hits me. I am so excited that I can barely talk. "Jesse..." I turn to him, my eyes wide and hopeful. "I think... I'm pregnant again."

His face lights up with joy. "Are you sure?"

Just like me, he dares not hope. But a mother knows. I've been nauseous before as a result of some food that I ate, but never like this. This is a special feeling, and my body immediately recognizes it.

I nod at him, and he sweeps me up in a bear hug, spinning me around, as I laugh with all my heart.

"We're finally going to have another baby!" he exclaims, settling me down and taking my face into his hands. "I can't believe it!"

I'm unable to suppress tears of joy. He notices them immediately and wipes them away with his thumb.

"We have to get a test," I tell him.

"Right now," he nods, grabbing me by the hand and pulling me back towards the car. "First stop, a pharmacy and then home to check."

"Sure," I chuckle.

"Then," he continues as we're flying back to the car, with people looking at us strangely, wondering where we're headed in such a rush. "We need to decorate the nursery again. Oh, and get Emma a new big sister t-shirt!" he exclaims with joy.

I can't stop smiling, my jaw almost stuck in this position. I can't believe how much Jesse has changed over the years. I had no doubts that he would be a good father. But when Emma came into our lives, even I was surprised how hands on he was with her. He wanted to do everything, from giving her a bath and changing a diaper to feeding her. It was an incredible bonding experience for us all, as a family, and I am so glad that we all got to experience it together.

Now, finally, we will be given another chance to repeat that miracle. It was almost unbelievable.

We buy a test on the way back, and we can't stop talking about this.

"Paisley," he suggests a name, as we're driving back home.

"Not bad," I nod. "I like flowers. Rose?"

"Too... ordinary," he frowns, keeping his eyes firmly fixated on the road. "Chrysanthemum?"

"Well, seriously now," I laugh at his suggestion, which is obviously a joke. "I know you can't be serious with that!"

"What?" he laughs. "We could call her Chrissy."

"Absolutely not," I can't stop laughing. "Something more ordinary, please."

"OK, that's if it's a girl," he changes the flow of the conversation. "What if it's a boy?"

I think about it for a moment. "No ordinary names?"

"Absolutely not," he shakes his head. "And no flowers for boys."

"OK, OK," I agree.

We continue our fun banter in the same direction, teasing each other, but at the same time trying to come up with good names that we might potentially use. Then, the conversation is somehow steered in the direction of managing two kids and how we'll organize everything.

"Two kids change everything," he tells me gravely. "It's different than one. Much different, I'm told."

"You mean, much better," I correct him.

"Sure," he chuckles. "Much more difficult as well, probably."

"But we're a team," I place my hand on his shoulder gently. "We can handle whatever it is."

"What if it's twins?" he suddenly asks.

I gasp. Then, I realize it doesn't matter. "Twice the fun then," I laugh.

When we get home, I immediately run upstairs to take a pregnancy test. I know he's sitting on the bed, just like he did last time, waiting nervously for me to come out.

I stare at the little strip, waiting for the revelation. Every second feels like a whole hour. My body is tingling, trembling. I am completely washed over by this hope.

What if it's a negative? I suddenly frighten myself with this question.

What if it's just a false alarm? What if I raised our hopes for nothing, only to dash them against the hard shores of reality?

I banish these thoughts from my mind, as I focus on the strip, waiting for it to change. Finally, it does.

I run out of the bathroom, holding the test in my hand, waving it victoriously in the air.

"It's a baby!" I shout. "I'm pregnant!"

His lips roll into a look of shock, surprise and delight, all wrapped up into one. We hug each other tightly, remaining embraced like that for a long time.

At that moment, we hear the doorbell, and we know who it is. We both run downstairs. Immediately upon opening the door, Jesse lifts Emma into his arms, and showers her sweet, freckled face with tender, butterfly kisses.

"Do you know we've got some news?" he tells her.

I hold the door open for Bobby, kissing him on the cheek. He looks at me, expectant, and I nod, gesturing that there really is something important to be shared.

"What is it, daddy?" Emma asks, her voice thin, as if she were a little mouse from a Disney cartoon.

"Mommy is having another baby," he announces, and both she and Bobby gasp with delight.

"Does that mean I'm going to be a big sister?" Emma exclaims with joy, clapping her little hands together.

"Yes, little lady," Jesse nods. "That means exactly that!"

All three of us hug, and Emma pretends like we're choking her, so we release her from our grip.

"Uncle Bobby!" She rushes over to him. "Did you hear that?"

"You mean, that I'll be twice an uncle? Yeah, that's great news!"

I walk over to him to accept his congratulations. "Those are really awesome news," he adds. "We'll have kids of a similar age. They'll get to play together and grow up together."

"That's wonderful," I nod, with a smile, already imagining how beloved that little baby will be, just like Emma is, and just like Bobby's child will be as well. "Why don't I make us some coffee, while you and Emma tell us how it was at the circus?"

"Oh, it was awesome!" Emma easily slides into this topic, ecstatic to share everything that they have seen. She spends the next half an hour talking about clowns, jugglers, magicians who performed card tricks and extracting bunnies out of their hats. Then, she continues with wild animals she has seen in the zoo, but it's of course, very different when you see them in the circus.

That night, none of us have trouble sleeping. We all doze off easily, and the following morning the joy simply extends. That is what happens in the following few months, until our doctor's appointment.

I am lying down on the doctor's bed, with my belly all lubed up. The screen is flickering black and white, and occasionally I can see faint outlines of a head or toes, but it quickly dissolves into a blur. The doctor keeps looking at the screen, noting something, when she finally turns to us, with a smile.

"Would you like to know the gender?" she asks.

"Of course, we have both names covered," Jesse replies first.

The doctor seems confused, then she continues. "You might need them both, because... you're having twins!"

"Twins!?" we exclaim at the same time, our voices merging together into a unity of shock, disbelief and absolute joy.

"We're having twins?" I ask again, my voice on the verge of breaking. I feel like I've been rewarded for all of my patience with not one baby, but two.

"Yes," the doctor smiles, pointing her finger at the screen. "See? Here is the girl, she has her little butt turned to us. A cheeky little thing, I can already see that. And your sweet little boy is asleep, sucking his thumb."

"They can do that, in there?" Jesse asks, incredulously.

"Of course," the doctor laughs. "That's where they learn it first and see if they like it or not."

Our appointment ends quickly after that, and we find ourselves in the car, seated, unable to move, or speak. Our minds need some time to process this information. Our lives will change. Nothing will ever be the same. But we're smiling. It's overwhelming to find out we're having twins, but at the same time, I feel like we couldn't be happier.

"Twins?" he turns to me.

"Twins," I reply, unable to stop smiling. "We got this... right?"

He takes my hand into his and brings it to his lips. "You know we do."

"Is this our happily ever after?" I ask again.

"No," he shakes his head at me, our fingers intertwined. "This is just the beginning. We continue it every single day, because it's not about the wedding day or some grand romantic gestures. It is about little things. It is about daily moments of love and affection, the love we share with each other, with Emma, and soon, with the twins."

He presses his free hand to my belly. I know exactly what he means, because our wedding was just the beginning. I feel like I've been falling in love with this man more and more as time went by. And there is no end to this love. It will last forever..

Enjoy what you read? Please leave a review!

Don't miss out!

Visit the website below and you can sign up to receive emails whenever Erica Frost publishes a new book. There's no charge and no obligation.

https://books2read.com/r/B-A-YRSV-YHNBF

BOOKS2READ

Connecting independent readers to independent writers.

Did you love *Ruthless Billionaire*? Then you should read *Billionaire Secrets*[1] by Erica Frost!

Grumpy billionaire boss. Game on. Nannying for billionaire grump Dominic Hart is putting me through school. Allowing me to become a lawyer one day. And ensure what happened to my dad won't happen again. Dominic Hart is nothing more than my boss. Who cares how suave he is. I'm not going to warm the bed of a man much older than me. Especially given how inexperienced I am. But the more time I spend with Dominic, the harder it is to resist. Until I don't. His kisses make me feel alive. His touch awakens my passion. Just as I start to fall for Dominic, he's accused of kidnapping his business competitor. If I help the police bury my boss, they'll reopen my father's case. But can I throw Dominic under the bus? I must choose between the man who raised me

---

1. https://books2read.com/u/3RlO8R

2. https://books2read.com/u/3RlO8R

and the one I'm falling for. Billionaire Secrets is a standalone New Adult Romance with a HEA and NO cheating!

Also by Erica Frost

Seduced By A Billionaire
Dark Secrets
A Billionaire's Game
Power Play
Ruthless Rival
Taming The Billionaire
The Hated Billionaire
3-Pointer
Baby For The Billionaire
My Best Friend's Brother
Ruthless Rival
The Comeback
Billionaire Corruption
Nannying For A Billionaire
The Billionaire's Surprise Baby
Accidental Love
Billionaire Secrets
Ruthless Billionaire

Milton Keynes UK
Ingram Content Group UK Ltd.
UKHW041822201024
449814UK00001B/71